The Roots of Poverty
in Latin America

The Roots of Poverty in Latin America

GUILLERMO M. YEATTS

Foreword by José Ignacio García Hamilton

McFarland & Company, Inc., Publishers
Jefferson, North Carolina, and London

Translated from the Spanish by Gabriela Mrad.

LIBRARY OF CONGRESS CATALOGUING-IN-PUBLICATION DATA

Yeatts, Guillermo M.
    The roots of poverty in Latin America / Guillermo M. Yeatts ; foreword by José Ignacio García Hamilton.
        p.   cm.
    Includes bibliographical references and index.

    ISBN-13: 978-0-7864-2235-7
    softcover : 50# alkaline paper ∞

    1. Latin America — Economic conditions.   2. Latin America — Economic policy.   3. Poverty — Latin America.   4. Economic development — Social aspects — Latin America.   5. Economic development — Sociological aspects.   I. Title.
HC123.Y4313   2005
339.4'6'098 — dc22   2005012776

British Library cataloguing data are available

©2005 Guillermo M. Yeatts. All rights reserved

No part of this book may be reproduced or transmitted in any form or by any means, electronic or mechanical, including photocopying or recording, or by any information storage and retrieval system, without permission in writing from the publisher.

Cover photograph © 2005 Photodisc

Manufactured in the United States of America

McFarland & Company, Inc., Publishers
  Box 611, Jefferson, North Carolina 28640
    www.mcfarlandpub.com

Contents

Foreword: The Scant but Valuable Tradition of Self-Examination
  by José Ignacio García Hamilton   1

1 — Poverty to the South of the Rio Grande   7
2 — Spain, Great Britain, and the Limits to Royal Power   18
3 — Public Conquest, Private Colonization   35
4 — Post-Independence Institutional Continuity in America   49
5 — Rebirth and Decline of Interventionist Institutions (1930–1990)   71
6 — The Rent-Seeking of the 1990s   87
7 — The Counter Reforms of the New Century   104
8 — Argentina: One Way Trip to Collapse   116
9 — Toward a Competitive Federalism   129
10 — Vested Interests Blocks Institutional Change   142
11 — A Way Out for Latin America   152

Notes   167
Bibliography   173
Index   177

Foreword:
The Scant but Valuable Tradition of Self-Examination

by José Ignacio García Hamilton

When one looks at a map of the American continent, it is evident that a geographical marker separates two diverse traditions. The Rio Grande serves as the divider between the United States and Mexico. To the North, progress and democracy have been on display for more than 200 years. To the South, dictatorships have alternated with budding democracies in an environment of stagnation and poverty, with a few occasional exceptions.

Poverty in Latin America has been studied from the most diverse angles—from the theory of the terms of exchange to the effects of climate, to political and social factors, to an inconsistent attempt at extending the theory of exploitation to the international sphere.

Guillermo M. Yeatts approaches this topic from a unique and profound perspective that uncovers the very roots of poverty. It analyzes the institutional, formal causes, such as laws and regulations, as well as the informal ones, such as work habits and cultural, religious, and social beliefs.

An understanding of the deep causes of stagnation is a necessary condition for finding lasting solutions rather than short-term fixes with transitory benefits. In addition, knowing the true causes will allow us to analyze the extent of the reforms currently underway in Latin America. Are they permanent changes that will allow these countries to bid farewell to stagnation, or are they mere circumstantial reforms with systemic defects that will lead to new crises?

When the Argentine dictator Juan Manuel de Rosas was deposed in

1852, the ideas of the young generation — exiled for almost 15 years — started to be heard and would eventually yield important political, social, economic, and cultural transformations. One such young man was Juan Bautista Alberdi, who in his *Bases y puntos de partida para la consolidación institucional*, written in Valparaiso, Chile, suggested to the first Argentine president, Justo José de Urquiza, that he convene a Constitutional Assembly, which met in the province of Santa Fe and, in 1853, enacted the National Constitution.

This seminal document incorporated republican principles that attempted to supersede three centuries of colonial culture. Hierarchical rankings were to be replaced by equality before the law; political absolutism, by the division of powers; religious uniformity, by freedom of worship; economic statism, by free trade; hatred for anything foreign, by the promotion of immigration; and the pervasive Hispanic-American practice of violation of the law, by the rule of law.

In those days, Mexico had overcome the extended period of the authoritarian rule of Antonio López de Santa Anna. In the Constitution of 1857 and the so-called *Leyes de Reforma*, classical liberals like Benito Juárez, Melchor Ocampo, and Santos Degollado managed to introduce similar notions to that country, in spite of the fight put up by traditional powers allied with the powerful Catholic church, which owned one-fifth of the country's wealth. To varying degrees, similar phenomena occurred in most countries in Spanish America.

In the Río de la Plata, these reforms generated formidable development, so much so that in the early decades of the twentieth century, Argentina was among the preeminent beef and grain exporters in the world and enjoyed political stability that seemed permanent.

In Mexico, the long tenure of Porfirio Díaz was responsible for substantial investment in railroads and other public works. Following the *Revolución Mexicana*, political democracy appeared to be a sure thing as well, and the large Latin American countries (as well as those geographically smaller like Uruguay and Chile) were expected to have a successful future and a prominent place in the modern world.

In those bountiful days, however, a handful of intellectuals sounded their warnings. The Argentine Juan Agustín García, in *La ciudad indiana*, wrote about the long absolutist tradition and its manifestation in the submission of *cabildos* to governors, as well as the generalized corruption arising from the violation of mercantile monopolies, which went so far as to involve monks in convents.

Another Argentine, Juan B. Terán from the province of Tucumán, in *El nacimiento de la América latina*, evoked the colonial culture of economic statism (land, mines, labor, and trade belonged to the state or depended on it) and the permanent disconnection between laws and reality. He warned against the rebirth of these colonial tendencies and of the bureaucratization of the first Radical administration, manifested in the high levels of public employment.

In contrast to the tone of these writings, in Uruguay, José Enrique Rodó published in 1900 his novel *Ariel*, which contained a memorable "Message to Youth" in which the virtues of Ariel were exalted as a symbol of the spirituality of culture, the morality of selflessness, the appreciation of art, and heroism. Confronting them were the defects of Caliban, who represented the sensuality of materialism, the emptiness of utilitarianism, and the error of bad taste.

Although in *Ariel* Rodó (unlike his French teacher Ernesto Renán) did not go so far as to disqualify sciences and democracy as responsible for "the outbreak of the utilitarian spirit," he still warned against the dangers of "democratic degeneration, which drowns in numbers any notion of quality; and dissolves in the conscience of societies any appreciation of order."

Rodó wrote about the dangers of an exaggerated admiration for the power and greatness of the United States and affirmed that Latin Americans have the "heritage of our race, a great ethnic tradition to uphold, a sacred bond that ties us to the immortal pages of our history." He acknowledged and lauded the United States experience in liberty, the cult of work and individual energy, the love for public instruction, the ability to apply scientific inventions, and the vocation toward action. But, like Herbert Spencer, he suggested that the country needed to change its course, abandoning utilitarian labor as the purpose of life and reclaiming the idealistic and contemplative idleness and moralizing leisure.

The culture of the United States—according to the Uruguayan author— gives its citizens a feeling of emptiness since their overriding concern is materialistic triumph and they subordinate their efforts to "the selfishness of personal and collective well-being." He added, "The cosmopolitan confusion and the atomism of a misunderstood democracy preclude the formation of a true national conscience."

Rodó predicted that the Yankees would not achieve preeminence, but that their positivism, represented by a sense of what was useful and by mechanical inventions, might one day become "intelligence, feeling, and idealism." He called on the youth of Hispanic America to participate in this transformation and spread around the world the altruistic and spiritual ideals—art, science, morality, religious sincerity—that is, the gospel of urbanity, intelligence, and selflessness. *Ariel* was a formidable literary success and continued to be widely read in high schools in Latin America throughout the twentieth century.

Another influential voice toward the end of the nineteenth century was that of José Martí, essayist, poet, and later martyr of Cuban independence, who, during his exile in New York, wrote "from the belly of the beast," criticizing North Americans as evil and greedy. Martí purported to be writing on behalf of the spiritual qualities of Latin Americans, which were the opposite of the obvious defects of North Americans.

In those days a Spanish writer said disdainfully, "Let them invent." His point was that scientific tasks and technological inventions were minor endeavors to be undertaken by the inferior Saxon peoples, while Hispanics were destined for higher spiritual tasks.

This view of their shared common past and the attitude of false superiority toward the cultures of the Protestant countries that had cultivated the capitalist spirit, religious tolerance, and political democracy had some bearing on the frustrated development of most former colonies of Spanish America, which reach the new millennium still plagued by unproductive and authoritarian elements.

Guillermo M. Yeatts, a man of action and of thought, has not added his voice to the intense nationalistic currents that, for example, in Mexico, blame Spain or the United States for any deficiency, past or present. In Mexico, the lack of self-examination has been emblazoned in the national Constitution: Section 33 punishes foreigners that dare criticize Mexican society. In Argentina, in the 1930s, the extended nationalistic movement accused British investment of having calamitous consequences, while the world observed the excellent level of progress that the country had enjoyed from 1853.

Yeatts has rejected xenophobic ideas, which put the blame on external problems, and which during the 1970s systematically condemned U.S. imperialism. In those days the Theory of Dependence was being developed in Latin America, which affirmed that the wealth of the central countries directly caused the poverty of peripheral nations. This formulation would eventually be renounced by some of its proponents (such as Brazilian president Fernando Henrique Cardoso); its assumptions are rigorously analyzed by the author of the present volume.

Guillermo M. Yeatts follows in the illustrious steps of Juan Agustín García and Juan B. Terán (and the Venezuelan Carlos Rangel, among others) and has given us a brilliant analysis of our societies, examining in depth the conflicts that plague our culture.

He offers a raw assessment of Latin American stagnation, seen through the lens of its Spanish past and contrasted lucidly with the path of the British and United States societies. The author exhibits a rare universalistic insight, with solid knowledge of Protestant and Catholic, Latin and Saxon societies, blended with more modern schools of thought, applied to a topic that is becoming increasingly difficult to ignore.

This book is serious, well documented, and captivating, and proves Yeatts to be an original and courageous essayist. He has picked up a scant but fruitful tradition in our continent, with substance and in the best intellectual style.

1
Poverty to the South of the Rio Grande

Can we explain the radical change in economic well-being when we step across the boundary between the United States and Mexico? — Douglass North[1]

There is a marked contrast between the quality of life of those who live in Latin American countries and those who live in the United States. In the same continent, divided only by the Rio Grande, an abyss seems to separate long-term economic growth from stagnation, success from failure, and, using ECLAC (United Nations Economic Commission for Latin America and the Caribbean) terminology, development from underdevelopment.

Two sets of institutions correspond to the two Americas: one Anglo-Saxon, the other Spanish-Portuguese; one prosperous, the other one poor. From an institutional point of view, America can be viewed as a "living laboratory," where a single geographic matrix hosts two different legacies, each with its own legal, administrative, economic, cultural, and religious baggage, each evolving on the *tabula rasa* that was the new continent, each obtaining distinct results.

Subsurface Wealth: The Struggle for Privatization in Argentina[2] described how the institutional framework in Argentina was responsible for the economic failure of the oil and gas industry; that analysis can be applied seamlessly to the rest of Latin America. The rights of the king (and later the state) to the riches in the subsurface constituted the cornerstone of a system that discouraged investment, risk-taking, and innovation. Institutions in place in the United States, based on the principle of private property rights to subsurface resources, encouraged exploration and exploitation of oil and gas, and the country became a world power in the industry. While in the United States anybody who finds oil in their property immediately becomes wealthy,³ whoever does so in Latin America not only does not become rich, but his property is all but taken over by the state or the recipient of the state's license to exploit the area.

An in-depth analysis of the institutions responsible for relegating the hydrocarbons sector in Latin America to stagnation sheds light on the rules of the game that precluded the continent from achieving economic growth. Further, it shows that the specific instance of the oil and gas industry was but the tip of a greater and deeper problem.

The present work sets out to analyze the role of institutions in Latin America, both formal (such as the legal framework) and informal (such as customs and religious values), and to determine how the prevailing rules in these societies generate incentives for creating and distributing wealth.

Society is ruled by norms. These can be written and legal, or cultural, religious and relating to uses and customs. The former are formal, issued by the legislature and can take the form of constitutions, statutes, decrees, codes, regulations, etc. They are written and their observance is enforced by a superior power. The latter are informal and are the result of cultural tradition — "habits" in the writings of Argentine intellectual Juan Bautista Alberdi — religion, personality, values that prevail in society, etc. There is no enforcement for these other than conscience, social punishment, and the desire for peaceful coexistence between persons. Except in the case of religion, there is no code that sets punishments for their violation.

Informal institutions limit the actions of men and women as much as formal ones do. In many cases, the informal ones predate the formal ones and came about as rules of coexistence. Arthur Shenfield wrote,

> The law, according to Hayek, is contemporary to society. The emergence of society is inconceivable without the development of rules of behavior. These can be considered uses or laws, but for a long time there was no distinction between the two words.... In particular, when a code or system was conceived to embody any concept of divine or natural law, the law was considered to have existed prior to its proclamation by a legislator. This is why the law was not the product of the will or the ideas of a legislator.⁴

Early on, the role of the state was to guard and administer the law, not to formulate it. Emperors and kings in medieval Europe, similarly, did not create the law, but were charged with defending it.

The precepts of formal and informal institutions started to diverge with the emergence of positivist legal theories. For positivists, law means legislation, legislation means sovereignty, and consequently, "law can only emanate from the sovereign power."⁵

These theories contradict history, which clearly shows the prevalence of rules and systems of behavior that have been observed as law but not created or enforced by a formal authority. Examples of this are the rules of commerce observed long before they were institutionalized into merchant law or, in present times, international law, where the existing rules and regulations are not controlled or enforced by any supranational power.

Formal and informal institutions can either be compatible or clash. They are compatible when they provide incentives for action toward the same direction. For example, institutions may establish a normative framework that guides behavior toward economic growth, favoring the pursuit of profit, individual initiative, limited government, or they may produce a framework that leads to economic stagnation.

In Argentina, during the period between the discovery of America and the enactment of the Constitution of 1853, Argentina's colonial informal rules coexisted with formal institutions. Economic and social results signaled continuous impoverishment, and by 1853 Argentina was a desert similar to the one the first colonists found upon arriving.

A second period, starting in 1853 and ending somewhere between 1918 and 1930, shows formal institutions undergoing an extreme transformation, to the point of openly contradicting the previous legal system. This change in rules brought about economic growth, restricted the power of government to specific functions, allowed the introduction of immigration and of foreign capital to the country, together with railroad lines, ports, and expansion of trade that would last for almost eight decades.

During the period from between 1918 and 1930 until the hyperinflation crisis of 1989, formal institutions (laws, decrees, and the amendments to the Constitution) were once again in line with colonial habits. A culture contrary to trade and individual progress was reflected in the public monopoly of all economic sectors, the growing dependence on public employment (which guaranteed stability instead of profitability), the closing of the economy to the outside world, and the boom of the welfare state. The economic results were years of stagnation and inflation.

Table 1-1 shows per capita GDP for selected countries in America. Countries to the north of the Rio Grande (United States and Canada) with Saxon legal and cultural roots fared better than Latin America. Although the per capita GDP is but one of many indicators, other measures would yield similar results.

But what factors have determined the meager economic performance in Latin America and abundant wealth in English America? In recent years, there has been a renewed interest in studying the overwhelming contrast between these societies, and several works have been written in an effort

TABLE 1-1
One Continent, Two Americas
Per Capita Gross Domestic Product (nominal) for Selected American Countries, 2004

Country	US$
United States	32,517
Canada	24,058
Argentina	6,928
Chile	5,576
Brazil	4,570
Mexico	3,631
Venezuela	2,970
Peru	2,379
Colombia	2,281

Source: *Index Economic Liberty 2005*, Heritage.

to find an answer. For instance, José Ignacio García Hamilton analyzes how political absolutism, militarism, violation of the law, economic statism, and religious fanaticism, among other factors, stand in the way of consolidating open, lay, productive societies with republican governments.[6] Mariano Grondona and Lawrence Harrison examine the close relationship between underlying values in developed and under-developed societies, and economic development.[7] The starting point of Harrison's approach is an analysis of the profound differences between the Spanish-Catholic culture and the Anglo-Protestant tradition, reflected in distinct views about work, education, merit, community, ethics, and authority, among other issues. Carlos Alberto Montaner, Plinio Apuleyo, and Alvaro Vargas Llosa — using a decidedly more journalistic approach — show how the ideas and attitudes of politicians, priests, military, business people, and unions keep Latin American masses in poverty as well as some pockets in Spain and other Mediterranean European regions.[8] Paul Craig Roberts and Karen Lafollette Araujo focus on how the region's economic reforms could signal a break with the traditions inherited from Spain, where networks of privileges are created, where markets for goods, services, and capital are suppressed through over-regulation, and a hostile attitude exists toward commerce and work.[9]

Perverse Rules, Perverse Results

In *Institutions, Institutional Change and Economic Performance*, Douglass North, recipient of the 1993 Nobel Prize in Economics, discusses his theory concerning the role of institutions in economic performance. Institutions are the rules of the game in a society or, more formally, they are "humanly devised constraints that shape human interaction" and affect the performance of the economy:

> Not all human cooperation is socially productive, of course; indeed, this study is concerned as much with explaining the evolution of institutional frameworks that induce economic growth and decline as with accounting for the successes.[10]

By institutions the author is referring to formal and informal limitations that condition human behavior, such as moral conscience and religion, customs and uses, civil and administrative organization, rules and regulations, and the prevailing economic-political doctrines. In *The Rise of the Western World. A New Economic History*, Douglass North and Robert Thomas described as efficient that set of institutions and property rights that encourages individual economic activity that produces private benefits and social ones in similar measure.[11]

Traditional theories of economic growth have considered technological change and investment in human capital to be the most powerful sources of economic growth in the western world. North and Thomas assert that neither innovation, economies of scale, education, nor capital accumulation are causes of growth but that they are growth itself. There can be no growth unless the existing economic organization is efficient and individuals have the necessary incentives to engage in socially desirable activities. Well-defined private property rights are the cornerstone of an economy that allows for the internalization of externalities and rewards or punishes individuals for their actions. As long as the actions of individuals are voluntary and free from governmental interference, they will tend to create an efficient allocation of resources.

To test their theory, North and Thomas look at the conditions in Spain and France and in England and Holland, toward the end of the Middle Ages and at the beginning of the Modern Age. They describe how the limitation — or the absence of limitation — of the royal power of the king conditioned the growth or stagnation of these nations and of the countries that inherited their institutional legacy.

A clear example of this is the contrast in *performance* of geographically similar nations, alluded to by historian David Rock. Rock explains that it was the Spanish occupation of Argentina in the sixteenth century that determined the evolution of cultural and economic institutions in that country, which otherwise might have developed in ways similar to those in Australia or Canada, countries with similar resources and whose economies developed at roughly the same time.[12]

Another Nobel Prize winner (1986), James Buchanan, studied the role of rules in determining whether the activities of economic agents will be socially beneficial. Buchanan distinguishes two types of economic behavior generated by two sets of rules: profit-seeking behavior and rent-seeking behavior. He defines the first one as that entrepreneurial behavior that obtains profits as a result of competition in an open market and by virtue of offering a better product at a lower price. In the second, benefits do not derive from meeting a need in a competitive context, but from a legal obstacle to competition, an artificial monopoly, a special permit, etc. For Buchanan, while in the first case both parties in the transaction benefit through free and voluntary exchange, in the second, one benefits at the expense of the other. The profit seeker is the real entrepreneur, whereas the rent seeker is a false entrepreneur, depending for his success on privileges granted by the state.

TABLE 1-2
Two Americas, Two Games

	Latin America	United States
Prevailing type of exchange	Involuntary	Voluntary
Government interference	High	Low
Type of game	Zero-sum	Win-win
Wealth	Fixed	Variable
Consequences of altering market signals	Resource allocation in activities that are unprofitable	Resource allocation follows social preferences
Economic activity	Fight for distribution of (fixed) wealth	Wealth creation
Type of social interaction	Conflict	Cooperation
Environment for negotiation	Government	Market
Economic behavior encouraged	Rent-seeking	Profit-seeking
Economic performance	Stagnation and poverty	Growth

The history of Latin America has been plagued with the second type of behavior. *Rent-seeking* is socially unproductive behavior in which in the short term one player wins, and the other one loses, but in the long term, everybody loses.

This was the prevailing behavior in the Iberian Peninsula. The alliance of rent-seeking sectors with the royal power resulted in anti-competitive policies such as restrictions on imports, grants of permits for mining exploitation, regulation of financial markets, etc. The king assigned himself the task of allocating resources, in exchange for fiscal benefits or revenue.

Eventually, state interference with individual decision-making and voluntary exchanges became a fundamental element of Latin American economic policies. The absence of limits to state action altered patterns of exchange among individuals as well as their relationship with the government, generating a perverse game in which the state took over the market's role of allocating resources. The mutual benefit that characterizes voluntary exchange was replaced by a distributive struggle, with the state acting as an intermediary or guarantor of involuntary transfers of wealth.

In *Law, Legislation and Liberty,* Friedrich von Hayek describes a practice that is common in Latin America — an organized group pursues or wields power toward securing private rents for its members. Such efforts produce conflict among different groups, fracturing society in the process.[13]

The history of Latin America is the history of the lack of limits on the actions of the King, and later of the national states, as well as that of the alliance between king-state and economic interest groups for the distribution of rents. In the economic sphere, the prevailing policies tended to provide greater benefits to a few with concentrated interests, with the costs falling on the majority of the population, whose interests were diffuse. These policies were implemented by means of redistributive fiscal policies, foreign policies that limited international trade, and a maze of economic regulations in the domestic market.[14]

The existence of a fixed level of wealth is an implicit assumption underlying the social behavior oriented toward obtaining a bigger slice of the total pie. In this game, the king/state is the legitimate arbiter that assigns slices according to its own discretion. On the other hand, the view that prevailed in the United States was that of wealth creation, according to which total wealth is variable and hinges on the ability of individuals to produce goods and services that meet the needs of others. In a strict sense, the outcome of the struggle for the distribution of wealth is the net destruction of value. Public choice theorist Gordon Tullock writes,

> In my youth, I spent some time in China. I was deeply impressed by the fact that a group of very energetic and intelligent people did not seem to be producing very much and hence had a very low living standard. A careful inspection turned up two obvious reasons for their relative poverty. First, there was a very large number of economic institutions which promoted inefficiency — government-sponsored monopoly, for example. Numerous and detailed regulations which not only created

monopolies but sharply reduced efficiency were also very common. Second, the principal economic activity of the more intelligent and better educated citizens was not actually producing things but attempting to achieve rents of one sort or another or at least to avoid exploitation by achieving the favor and special consideration of the government. It was obvious that this activity, although personally profitable, was socially unproductive.[15]

It is quite remarkable that the absence of limitations to state intervention, far from generating repulsion and conflicts with the population, has been validated repeatedly by popular elections and, in periods when administrations were autocratic, by implicit consensus. Intellectuals, businessmen, politicians, and the public at large did not repudiate the lack of limits to government interference. Moreover, they applauded it and attempted to benefit from it.

It is a common practice in Latin America, in order to remedy the effects of a statute or regulation that violates private property rights of one group, to pass another statute or regulation that in turn will infringe on the rights of a third group. Rarely will a set of rules be enacted that limits state jurisdiction over property rights. If the fundamental elements of the market process are private property and the right to use and dispose of it, true markets have not existed in Latin America, since private property has been subjected to the arbitrariness of political power since its early days.

In contrast, predominant institutional traditions in the United States have been characterized by voluntary exchanges, free from government interference. The development of exchange as win-win games enabled the development of a society based on authentic market signals resulting from the preferences of individuals.

From the discovery of America up until the 1990s, repeated attempts at state reform in former Spanish colonies have shared the same imprimatur. The absence of voluntary exchanges has manifested itself in the most diverse institutions, from the Spanish monopolistic system, to state interventionism prior to World War II, to the "privatizations" of the last decade that transformed state-owned corporations into legal monopolies.

Law Versus Morality = Corruption

The dominant position in Latin America was—and still is—that rules are external to the individual. The king or state and religion made the rules with which individuals had to comply, not by choice but by dogma.

What was "good" and "bad" was determined prior to their decision. Far from the moral imperatives of Immanuel Kant in his *Critique of Practical Reason*, defined as subjective and self-imposed rules set by each individual, the concept of morality prevailing in Latin America was an objective one, a single and absolute morality that excluded alternatives. In the Anglo-Saxon tradition, especially since the Protestant reform, the predominant notion was one of moral autonomy, understood as the prevalence of one's personal rules emanating from the exercise of free will. In the context of freedom of choice, and in a process of trial and error, individuals become responsible for their own actions. "Good" actions are rewarded and "bad" ones punished. This becomes law — one's own law. In the economic sphere, the internalization of profits and losses resulting from one's own actions generates incentives for efficiency, creativity, and innovation, and this is the basis for good customs and habits in the moral sphere. In a free society, there is no gap between individual and social rules.

When there is a gap between individual morality and statutes or external rules, the individual faces a difficult dilemma, in which personal beliefs tend to prevail. In the nineteenth century, the French economist Frédéric Bastiat commented on the consequences of separating law and morality:

> No society can exist unless the laws are respected to a certain degree. The safest way to make laws respected is to make them respectable. When law and morality contradict each other, the citizen has the cruel alternative of either losing his moral sense or losing his respect for the law. These two evils are of equal consequence, and it would be difficult for a person to choose between them.[16]

Such was the effect of the normative hypertrophy of Latin American legislation, which resulted in "legitimate corruption," as individuals, in their daily struggle to survive, ignored some of the numerous rules sanctioned by the king/state. The responses to elevated taxation were evasion, protectionism, smuggling, regulation, "black markets," bribes, and their many byproducts. As a result of legal oppression and having to live under stringent rules, rich and unplanned institutions evolved spontaneously that allowed a quasi–Darwinian adaptation of man to hard social conditions.

In *The Other Path*, Hernando de Soto illuminates the effects on his native Peru of the contradictions between morality and law — an example that can be easily extended to the rest of Latin America. In the foreword to *The Other Path*, Mario Vargas Llosa explains the origin of the informal economy as the cruel alternative between observing the law and respecting moral precepts as instruments of survival. When the law makes it all but impossible for the masses to achieve even moderate economic success, they reject the law and seek economic opportunity outside it.[17]

In Latin America, the informal sector functioned along the lines of an intuitive application of the right to resist oppression enunciated by John Locke in 1688.[18] The absence of limitations to royal power and, later, to the power of Latin American nation states, led to the proliferation of regulations and other forms of state intervention that materially restricted the exercise of rights enunciated in their respective constitutions.

In order to satisfy both the individual's own conscience and social norms, divergent behaviors evolved and coexisted on many levels: respect for laws and corruption, marriages that could not be dissolved and infidelity, formal federalism and centralized administration of resources. The origins of the systematic violation of rules in Latin America may be traced at least partially to this double normative system.

In the specific case of Argentina, regulatory norms that ruled the economy since the early days of the republic, and especially those enacted in the 1940s, generated a set of incentives that fostered informality. Regulation — and taxation — made the opportunity cost of operating in the formal sector increasingly expensive. The cost of belonging to the formal economy is the counterpart to the benefits of informality. The more regulations there are, the higher the benefit from evading them. It is in pursuit of that benefit that individuals adopt informal behaviors. This process is accelerated when the cost of regulations is so high that it precludes participation in the legal sector. That is why Vargas Llosa concludes that many of those participating in the informal sector were literally expelled from the legal markets.

Is There an End to the Latin American Vicious Cycle?

The history of Latin America is the history of its poverty and that of its peoples. The 1980s have been referred to as the lost decade. Recurring domestic fiscal crises damaged the image of the region abroad. The 1990s were a decade of economic reform, with varying degrees of progress and impact for most countries in the region. As the new century begins, both popular opinion and statements made by business and union associations again wish for the good old times gone by. In the political sphere, old practices prevail (electoral systems that favor closed access to political life, electoral fraud, public service as unemployment subsidy, corruption, etc.). In the economy, once fiscal crises are tamed, public spending grows again, as do fiscal pressure and public debt.

On the other hand, openness and competition are generating new and more efficient behavior patterns that slowly seem to be chipping away at the centuries-old institutions of failure. Corporations like McDonald's have started to instill in youth the pride of working and creating value by serving the customer. Only a few years ago, young people had but one way open to them: to apply for a job in the public sector, with no responsibility for their actions, reward for their efforts, or punishment for their laziness. In the best of cases, some of them could secure jobs in a state corporation or a company whose position was protected by high import duties or other such restrictions, or a firm in a monopolistic or oligopolistic position with limited competition in the domestic market.

Countries like the United States, where rules are internalized and observed, enjoy a climate of certainty and lower transaction costs. In Latin America, changes in rules, tax evasion, and violation of the rules are part of the game, and the resulting uncertainty discourages healthy economic activity. Formal institutions (legal framework, statutes, and other laws, although not the constitutions) have been responsible for behavior that ran against economic development. Informal institutions (culture, customs, moral and religious prejudices) have contributed to the situation.

With the new reforms in Latin America as the background for the inquiry, this essay will explore the following questions: How have formal institutions influenced the economic development of the region? Have customs, uses, and religious values been constraints or engines for economic growth? Do the reforms of the 1990s represent true institutional change? Is it possible to end the vicious cycle of underdevelopment? Is there a way to break the cycle? Is there hope for a different future?

2
Spain, Great Britain, and the Limits to Royal Power

> *In the greater part of Spain, around 1476, no one could say "this is mine" and "this is yours," for the luck of a battle, the favor of the sovereign, a change of sides, were enough to cause a person's property to be confiscated and given to someone else. It was a state of general chaos.* — Jaime Vicens Vives[19]

It is not correct to say that the institutional history of America began in 1492, with the discovery of the new continent. It took centuries to develop the uses, values, and rules that would eventually make it to the continent upon discovery. Two different institutional traditions were evolving in the Iberian Peninsula and in the British Isles.

The geographical characteristics of the British Isles had helped prevent foreign invasions and fostered a peaceful climate; defense issues were not a priority for the kingdom and its subjects. The essential concern in the years that preceded the discovery of America was limiting the absolute power of the king to enable the expansion of individual liberties. The Magna Carta of 1215, the *Bill of Rights*, and the Glorious Revolution of 1688 are landmarks in this history of limiting monarchic power.

The New World witnessed the birth of two Americas that were diametrically opposed in their values, customs, and the rules that governed them. Iberian America saw the transfer of a consolidated monarchical absolutism. The institutions of English America, on the other hand, evolved as a consequence of the search for liberties initiated in the previous century.

Douglass North writes that "a traditional explanation for European success in contrast to China, Islam or other areas is competition amongst political units. There can be little doubt that this competition is an important part of the story, but clearly not the whole story. Parts of Europe failed to develop, Spain and Portugal stagnated for centuries and economic growth in the rest of Europe was uneven at best. It was the Netherlands and England that were the carriers of institutional change."[20]

Consolidation of Royal Power in Spain

By the sixteenth century, from an institutional perspective, England and Spain had developed substantially differently. England had evolved into a relatively centralized feudalism, product of the Norman conquest, and the House of Tudor was in power after the success in the Battle of Bosworth (1485).

In Spain, eight centuries of Moor dominion came to an end, having left deep footprints in the social, political, and economic reality of the Iberian Peninsula. Spain and Portugal embarked on the discovery and conquest of America "with the sensibility and tenor of the Reconquest. Nothing more original occurred to Cortes's soldiers amazed by the temples and pyramids of the Mayans and Aztecs, than to compare them with the mosques of Islam."[21] The Islamic influence impregnated in the core of the Spanish policies was an essential component of the conquest of the New World.

> Conquest and evangelization: these two words, deeply Spanish and Catholic, are also deeply Muslim. Conquest means not only the occupation of foreign territories and the subjugation of their inhabitants, but also the conversion of the conquered. The conversion legitimized the conquest. This politico-religious philosophy was diametrically opposed to that of English colonizing; the idea of evangelization occupied a secondary place in English colonial expansion.[22]

The predominant values and social rankings in Spanish society were related to military power, which also meant a lesser role for commercial activities. Also, the presence of a foreign enemy was the proper ground for the emergence of absolute values in building a single political and religious unit (Christians against Muslims).

José I. García Hamilton wrote about the close ties between the nobility, the military, and land ownership. With the Spanish kingdoms at war with the Moors, military assistance was a tremendous value. Success in battle was therefore rewarded with land and feudal power, and therefore, those with military might became nobility.[23]

Toward the end of the Middle Ages, the political, religious and economic organization of Spain continued to be profoundly medieval. Lines between State and Church, between public and private, were blurred. The relationship between politics and religion simplified the vigilance of the *Santo Oficio* during the Inquisition.[24] Contrary to developments in Britain, kings continued to enjoy absolute power and the growing revenues flowing in from the New World were assigned to political ends. Octavio Paz explains how dynastic alliances and monarchial suppression of freedoms persisted in Spain, while elsewhere the seeds of democracy took root.[25]

The situation in the Iberian peninsula was not homogeneous in terms of limitation of royal power. The union of Aragon — which included the territories of what are today Valencia, Aragon, and Catalonia — and Castile brought together two very diverse regions. Castile was continually involved in wars, whether against the Moors, or internally; and even when the *Cortes* existed, they were seldom convened. The centralized monarchy and bureaucracy of Castile defined the institutional evolution of both Spain and Spanish America. Aragon had been reconquered by the Arabs in the second half of the thirteenth century and had become a great commercial power encompassing Sardinia, Sicily, and parts of Greece. *Cortes* emerged that reflected rights obtained by subjects and that generally provided a secure environment for commercial and business developments. The union of the two kingdoms, far from being a balanced one, was essentially the supremacy of Castile over Aragon and its institutions:

> In the fifteen years after their union, Isabella succeeded in gaining control not only over the unruly warlike barons, but over church policy in Castile as well. Although the role of the Castilian Cortes has, in recent scholarly work, been somewhat upgraded, nevertheless there was a centralized monarchy and bureaucracy in Castile, and it was Castile that defined the institutional evolution of both Spain and Latin America.[26]

Even though the Magna Carta is among the earliest precedents for constitutional limits on monarchs, earlier institutional precedents for the limitation of royal power can be found in what is today Spain. Among them the *fueros* of León (1020), Jaca (1064), Nájera (1076), Toledo (1085), Burgos (1073), Calatayud (1120), Zaragoza (1115), Puebla de Organzón (1191), and in particular the Ordenamiento de León or Pacto de Sobrabe (1188), agreed to by King Alphonse I; this document includes some liberties that can be deemed early versions of principles recognized in modern constitutions.

Segundo Linares Quintana wrote that the *fueros* of Aragon of 1283 are an invaluable precedent for the modern notion of the supremacy of the constitution and the protection of individual rights.[27] The *fuero* was a supreme law that had to be obeyed by both the subjects and the king himself. Norberto Gorostiaga wrote that "the *fueros* had the rank of supreme law and were above the will of the king. Any actions by the king that contradicted the *fuero* were null and could not be applied. The same was true for any decisions by officials or judges, they were *ipso foro*."[28] Linares Quintana adds that in Aragon, the *juicio de manifestación* was a guarantee of physical liberty whose efficacy or technique were comparable to more modern guarantees.

Fiscal Voracity and Undefined Property Rights

In Spain, a large bureaucracy administered the ever-growing body of decrees and legal norms that set the course of action and at the same time legitimated the administrative machine.[29] The Crown's control over the economy is reflected in this passage from Jan De Vries's study of Europe:

> A whole school of economic reformers, the *arbitristas*, wrote mountains of tracts pleading for new measures.... Indeed, in 1623 a *Junta de Reformacion* recommended to the new king, Phillip IV, a series of measures including taxes to encourage earlier marriage (and, hence, population growth), limitations on the number of servants, the establishment of a bank, prohibitions on the import of luxuries, the closing of brothels, and the prohibition of the teaching of Latin in small towns (to reduce the flight from agriculture of peasants who had acquired a smattering of education). But no willpower could be found to follow through on these recommendations.... It is said that the only accomplishment of the reform movement was the abolition of the ruff collar, a fashion which had imposed ruinous laundry bills on the aristocracy.[30]

All the details of the economy and the polity were carefully structured to promote the interest of the Crown toward creating the most powerful Empire since Rome. But with the uprising in Holland and the decline of bullion flow from the New World, fiscal needs greatly exceeded income, and the result of the imbalance were bankruptcies, higher domestic taxes, confiscations, and insecure property rights.

The *mesta* is another example of the lack of definition of property rights. It was an institution by which exclusive grazing rights were granted by the king of Spain to the guild of sheepmen; these rights interfered with the private properties of third parties who used the land for growing crops.

Under the *mesta*, a landowner that had carefully planted his land at any moment could expect his crops to be eaten or destroyed by migratory flocks. The *mesta* contributed large amounts of resources to the treasury. By maintaining the institution largely for fiscal reasons, agricultural activities were discouraged.

Insecure property rights and an unpredictable tax system for financing the growing expenses of military adventures put Spain in a difficult position. In *The Rise of Western World. A New Economic History*, Douglass North writes that of the three major revenue resources of the Spanish Crown—the *mesta*, the payments from the Low Countries and other territories, and the treasures of the New World—two were external and helped define its destiny. External resources were a growing source of income, which not only explains the growth of Spanish political power and the great Habsburg Empire under Charles V and Philip II, but also its decline under Philip III and Philip IV as those resources declined.

The attempt by Charles V (1517–1556)—continued by Philip II—to establish a universal and Catholic monarchy proved extremely onerous. The expenses needed to maintain the house of cards they built grew every year, continuously exceeding revenues. The independence of the seven northern Dutch Provinces toward the end of the seventeenth century was another blow to the Crown's budget, and attempted to offset the loss with increases in the largest domestic taxes—the *alcabala* and the *millones*.

North writes that, as the financial difficulties of the Crown grew, embargos, confiscations, and interference with contracts became common, and people started to abandon productive activities. Economic stagnation was the inevitable consequence. In his paper *The Decline of Spain*, J. Elliot wrote, "The nature of the economic system was such that one could only aspire to be a scholar or a monk, beggar or bureaucrat. There were no other options."[31] On this subject, Douglass North wrote,

> War, the church, and administering the complex bureaucratic system provided the major organizational opportunities in Spain and in consequence, the military, priesthood, and the judiciary were rewarding occupations. The expulsion of the Moors and Jews, rent ceilings on land and price ceilings on wheat, confiscations of silver remittances to merchants in Seville (who were compensated with relatively worthless bonds called *juros*) were symptomatic of the disincentives to productive activity.[32]

Both the monarchies in England and Spain faced the need for additional revenue to support the increasing costs of the war. Traditionally, the king lived off the revenue from his estates together with feudal dues; but these resources were not sufficient given the new military technology associated with the use of the crossbow, longbow, pike, and gunpowder. The fiscal crises forced kings to bargain with their subjects.[33] As a consequence, a form of representation was established by the latter: the Parliament and the *Cortes* in Spain.

The outcomes of the crises were very different: in England, crisis led to political and economic developments that would come to dominate the Western world. In Spain, in spite of more favorable initial conditions, the results were fiscal crises, bank bankruptcies, confiscation of assets, insecure property rights, and the beginning of three centuries of relative stagnation. In the seventeenth century Spain went from being the most powerful nation in the world since the Roman Empire to being a secondary power. The depopulation of the fields, the stagnation of industry, and the collapse of the trade system between Seville and the New World combined with political events like the revolts of Catalonia and Portugal. According to North, the measures that were considered viable in terms of institutional limitations were price controls, higher taxes, and repeated confiscations.[34]

Limits to Power in England

While in Spain monarchic absolutism was reaching its highest point, in an England isolated from continental influences a different tradition was evolving. The institutional history of great Britain reflects the struggle to limit royal power. Even the migration of the pilgrims to America in search of religious freedom represents a stage in the pursuit of less interference by the king in the lives of citizens.

The English institutions were the result of a slow and gradual evolution of customs, and not of abstract theory. Constitutionalist A.V. Dicey wrote,

> [The English constitution] was not made but grown; it was the fruit not of abstract theory but of that instinct which (it is supposed) has enabled Englishmen and especially uncivilized Englishmen, to build up sound, lasting institutions, much as bees construct a honeycomb, without undergoing the degradation of understanding the principles on which they raise a fabric more subtly wrought than any work of conscious art ... no precise date could be named as the day of its birth; no definite body of persons could claim to be its creators, no one could point to the document which contained it s clauses.... [35]

In the English tradition rules did not emanate from the royal will nor were rights expressed in a positive sense, through extensive and detailed codes. Relations among private individuals were free and guided by unwritten, negative norms evolved from uses and customs. The set of rules that developed in England is known as the common law. As important a landmark as the Magna Carta of 1215 was in English law, it simply recognized pre-existing rights that had been acknowledged by court judgments based on the uses and customs incorporated into the common law. Judge Ricardo M. Rojas writes in this regard,

> To a large extent, the [Magna] Carta was just the royal recognition of a law already elaborated and applied since the times immemorial. This is evident in the frequent reference to uses or rules that did not arise by imposition but by spontaneous evolution.... Both Section 39 of the Magna Carta and section 31 of the Articles of the Barons signed on the same year, recognized the rights of merchants to buy and sell, to move and enter and leave England without paying any fees according to the ancient and fair customs [Articles of the Barons] or to ancient and permitted customs [Magna Carta].[36]

The *common law*, recognized by the king, limits the role of rules to the resolution of disputes among private parties and does not emulate the attempts at social engineering that were a feature of Continental European law. U.S. Supreme Court Justice Oliver W. Holmes, Jr., wrote,

> The life of the law has not been logic; it has been experience. The felt necessities of the time, the prevalent moral and political theories, intuitions of public policy, avowed or unconscious, even the prejudices which judges share with their fellow men have had a good deal more to do than the syllogism in determining the rules by which men should be governed. The law embodies the story of a nation's development through many centuries and it cannot be dealt with as if it contained only the axioms and corollaries of mathematics.[37]

Although England had neither codified statutes nor a written constitution it was a pioneer in the protection of individual rights and guarantees. English constitutionalists Chalmers and Hood Phillips wrote that in general constitutions include abstract declarations about rights but seldom provide remedies for violation; but in England, individual rights are deduced from judgments made by the courts in particular cases in which victims of the rights violation found redress. That is why they maintain that in England the rights preceded the law, and there is no law without its corresponding guarantee.[38]

Antecedents to Modern Constitutionalism

The Magna Carta signed on June 15, 1215 is one of the most important precedents to constitutionalism. King John made concessions and obligated his heirs to the agreement:

> To all free men of our kingdom we have also granted, for us and our heirs forever, all the liberties written out below, to have and to keep for them and their heirs, of us and our heirs....

Another clause established that "no free man shall be seized or imprisoned, or stripped of his rights or possessions or outlawed or exiled or deprived of his standing in any other way ... except by the lawful judgment of his equals or the law of the land." This text is considered a precedent for *habeas corpus* and *due process of law*. Toward the end of the document, a committee of barons is established to cause the document to be observed by the King.

Another important precedent is the *Agreement of the People* prepared in 1647, at a crucial moment in the Puritan revolution, by Oliver Cromwell's war council. It was not sanctioned by the House of Commons and was, consequently, not enforceable. Its relevance lies in that it had been intended as a supreme law of the land, limiting the powers of Parliament and stating expressly which rights the citizens hold for themselves — the violation of which by any authority would constitute a crime.[39] It also influenced the Instrument of Government, which Cromwell managed to get enacted on December 16, 1653. The Instrument provided for a Lord Protector, a Council of State, a single-chamber Parliament, and even includes the fundamental rights of the *Agreement of the People*.

TABLE 2-1
Legal Systems in the English and Spanish Traditions[40]

Feature	Spanish Legal System	English Legal System
Origin of the rules	Royal decree	Uses and customs recognized by courts
Purpose of the rules	Establish rights	Protect rights
Type of rules	Positive	Negative
Rules embodied in	Codes	Common law
Limits to rules	The will of the sovereign	Uses and customs as interpreted by judges

The open nature of British institutions, in stark contrast with continental Europe, favored the development of a different institutional tradition, one based in impersonal interactions, which is described by Douglass North as required for a stable political framework as well as to reap the economic benefits of emerging technologies. In Spain, political and economic interactions were largely based on personal relationships, with correspondingly different economic effects.[41]

The nature of *common law* rules was negative, that is, they simply stated those behaviors that were not permitted (according to judicial precedent), which enabled the evolution of a legal order based on free and voluntary agreements among individuals. Friedrich von Hayek wrote that this judge-made law was the result of the settlement of conflicts among individuals involved and so was unrelated to any other individual action that did not affect third parties. The domain reserved to each person was defined in this way, where third parties were not allowed to trespass. It served as a system to avoid conflicts among persons who did not act under a central plan but pursued their own ends to the best of their ability.[42]

While the purpose of the common law was to protect existing rights, Spanish continental law sought to establish rights. The role of the judges was to defend individuals against the arbitrariness and oppression of the State.

John Locke and the Struggle for Liberty

From the moment the Stuarts came to power, England was involved in permanent convulsion. Political passions were inflamed further by the religious fights between Protestants and Catholics, and among Protestants themselves (Anglicans and Puritan dissidents). In 1642, Charles Stuart I and Parliament—mostly made up of Puritans—undertook an armed conflict that ended with the dethronement and execution of the king by Cromwell's Parliamentary army, and the establishment of the Republic. The enthusiasm of the new government was quickly dampened by the religious fights and the serious political problems manifested by the struggle between *Tories* and *Whigs*. The Tories were the absolutist party, advocating the divine right of kings, and non-resistance to the power and will of the monarch. The Whigs favored limited monarchy and the power of Parliament. The Anglican church sided with the Tories and defended the royal power of the Stuart monarchs; after the revolution prevailed, the church was forced to acknowledge wide freedom of religion.

Cromwell's republic could not hold on for long and had to give way to the Restoration of Charles Stuart II. Upon his death in 1685, the king was succeeded by his brother James who unambiguously declared his Catholic faith, openly challenging the deepest feelings of a majority of the English people.[43]

The natural discontent with the king made the English people and the Anglican Church invite William of Orange to set up a new government. William's fleet of 600 ships landed on English shores in November of 1688, bringing 15,000 Dutch soldiers. The flag of the Prince of Orange defended liberty, Protestant religion, and Parliament. With the Stuarts easily dethroned, Parliament, Protestantism, and liberalism triumphed over absolutism and conservatism. The Glorious Revolution of 1688 meant the success of Whigs over Tories.

The "divine right of kings" had served as an excuse for the despotic and arbitrary behavior of the Stuart monarchs during the final years of their reign. The courts decided many cases unfairly, and taxes were raised considerably. All of these developments troubled the new merchant and industrial class who had gotten used to acting independently and had risen politically and economically. The freedoms they required to consolidate their positions could only be attained by eliminating absolutism. The historical and political events that gave England the opportunity to dispel the notion of the divine rights of kings found their support in the writings of John Locke.

The main elements of the Lockean thesis are respect for the individual, the concern for validating the Revolution of 1688, and the notion of a society organized for the benefits of its members. Locke justified the legitimacy of William II's ascension to the throne by popular consent, based on his natural law theory. Implied in his writings is the exaltation of the English Constitution based on the concepts of the end of the state of nature and the delegation of sovereignty.

In *Two Treatises of Government*, Locke developed his theory of the State, elaborating on the foundations of political association (from there the name civil government), limiting its purview, and establishing the conditions for its creation and dissolution. The basic tenet underlying his work is "anti-absolutism," the desire for political power limited by popular consent and natural law and eliminating the risk of despotism and arbitrariness inherent in the doctrine of the divine right of kings.

The anti-absolutist position, a negative concept, translates in his book into the positive fundamental thesis that government was created by the people with the purpose of ensuring their own well-being. For Locke, the existence of individuals' rights, including the right to private property, in the state of nature will protect them from abuses of power in the later societal state. In Locke's state of nature, natural law establishes that the natural reason "teaches all mankind who will but consult it, that being all equal and independent no one ought to harm another in his life, health, liberty or possessions."[44]

Locke's opposition to absolutism is clearly expressed in the following paragraph:

> Yet such have been the disorders ambition has filled the world with, that in the noise of war, which makes so great a part of the history of mankind, this consent is little taken notice of; and, therefore, many have mistaken the force of arms for the consent of the people, and reckon conquest as one of the originals of government. But conquest is as far from setting up any government as demolishing a house is from building a new one in the place. Indeed, it often makes way for a new frame of a commonwealth by destroying the former; but, without the consent of the people, can never erect a new one.[45]

He justifies the transition from the state of nature to the state of society by consent:

> Men being, as has been said, by Nature all free, equal, and independent, no one can be put out of his estate and subjected to the political power of another without his own consent, which is done by agreeing with other men to join and unite into a community for their comfortable, safe, and peaceful living, one amongst another, in a secure enjoyment of their properties and the greater security against any that are not a part of it.[46]

The people hold the real sovereign power and deposit it in the political authority; it is not an agreement of submission. The people will judge whether those in whom power has been deposited are using it to the benefit of society. Locke justifies the use of force by society when government loses legitimacy. This is the right to resist tyranny. Locke supported the right of the English revolutionaries and wanted to quiet the consciences of his compatriots, tormented after deposing James II.

The Spirit of Capitalism

The Reformation, initiated in the sixteenth century by Martin Luther, had enormous repercussion on the politics and religion of Europe. Politically, the Reformation debilitated the theory of the two swords, by which the Pope had political and religious control, agreeing to the appointment of new kings. From then on, kings would become defenders of the sovereignty and independence of states, deriving their power directly from God, without intermediaries. In opposing the Supremacy of the Pope and distributing ecclesiastical jurisdiction among the various communities, the Reformation had a decentralizing effect on the Church.

Linares Quintana affirms that the Reformation destroyed the idea of unity between Church and Empire and territorially reorganized Europe into different national states. From then on, religion and politics stopped being one unit. Before the Reformation, giving support to rulers was an article of faith, while the defense of a different religious creed was considered an attack against a ruler. The Reformation implied not only the right to dissent with the ruling government, but also possibly the right to resist it in the interest of what dissidents considered the true religion.[47]

Morally, the Reformation allowed greater freedom of conscience, and the individual acquired substantial and permanent value as a person. In this doctrinal contribution of the sixteenth century lie the philosophical foundation of liberty and the principles of self-government.[48] Raymond Gettel wrote that the Reformation had positive results for individual liberty because Reformers openly proclaimed equality among all men. When they attacked the hierarchy of the Church, they liberated the individual and made him answer only to God. They opposed the principle of authority and demanded wide freedom of conscience. In his treatise *De la libertad del hombre cristiano*, Luther wrote,

> One thing, and only one is necessary for Christian life: honesty and liberty. Neither the bishop nor the Pope, nor any other man has the right to impose a syllable of a law on a Christian without his consent; and whoever does, will do so under the spirit of tyranny.[49]

The religious Reformation coincided with attempts to limit absolute royal power in the political sphere. The rules of the new doctrines accompanied the emerging capitalist activities. German sociologist Max Weber, in *The Protestant Ethic and the Spirit of Capitalism*, analyzes in depth the relationship between the precepts of emerging religions and the capitalist behavior of the societies that held them.

Weber wrote that the desire to acquire wealth has existed in many societies in history. Capitalism so defined existed in Babylon and ancient Egypt, China, and medieval Europe. But only in Western society and in relatively recent times has capitalism been associated with the rational organization of the labor force and the systematic investment of capital.[50] The continued multiplication of capital, which demands the investment and reinvestment of profits, is alien to traditional types of enterprise. Businessmen associated with the development of rational capitalism combine the impulse toward accumulation with a frugal lifestyle.

Weber finds the answer in the asceticism of Puritanism, seen through the idea of a "calling." This notion was introduced by the Reformation; it existed neither in Antiquity nor in the Catholic theology. It refers to the idea that the highest form of moral obligation is completing one's tasks in earthly endeavors. This projects an ideal of religious behavior on daily life in contrast with the monastic ideal of Catholicism, which sought to transcend the worldly existence. Moreover, the moral responsibility of the Protestant is cumulative; the cycle of sin, repentance, and pardon that is constant in the life of the Catholic is absent in Protestantism.

Although the idea of a "calling" was already present in Luther's doctrine, Weber states that it was more rigorously developed in various Puritan sects, like Calvinism, Methodism, Pietism, and Baptist. A large portion of his study is devoted to the Calvinist doctrine of Predestination, by which some human beings were chosen by God for salvation and this had to be proved with success in daily undertakings. According to Weber, the capitalist spirit was born from this revolution.

The literature has abundant examples of the relationship between Protestant values and capitalist prosperity. Some might extend this to say there is a relationship between Catholic values and lower economic growth. Yet counterexamples cast doubt on religion as a determinant of growth. The cities of what is today Northern Italy (Florence, Milan among others) achieved prosperity while sharing those very religious values. But in sharp contrast to the Iberian Peninsula, their high level of cultural and economic development was based on a decentralized system that shared neither the values nor the political regime of Spain. Moreover, growth in Argentina between 1853 and 1930 shows that a country with a strong Catholic foundation may sustain long periods of economic growth given appropriate institutional modifications.

Octavio Paz contrasts the English and Spanish notions of work. In New Spain, work was not valued for itself, and in fact, leisure was a more noble pursuit. Wealth was valued mainly for its usefulness in waging war and building temples (p. 364). The Puritans, in contrast, valued work for its redemptive and purifying qualities.[51]

Paz also wrote about the differences between the Catholic and Protestant religions that the colonies would inherit:

> Both societies were religious, but their religious attitudes were irreconcilable.... One society fostered the complex and majestic conceptual structure of orthodoxy, an equally complex ecclesiastical hierarchy, wealthy

and militant religious orders, and a ritualistic view of religion, in which the sacraments occupied a central place. The other, fostered free discussion of the Scriptures, a small and often poor clergy, a tendency to eliminate the hierarchical boundaries between the simple believer and the priest, and a religious practice based not on ritual but on ethics, and not on the sacrament but on the internalizing of faith.

If one considers the historical evolution of the two societies, the main difference seems to be the following: the modern world began with the Reformation, which was the religious criticism of religion and the necessary antecedent of the Enlightenment; with the Counter-Reformation and Neo-Thomism, Spain and her possessions closed themselves to the modern world.... And so, though Spanish American civilization is to be admired on many counts, it reminds one of a structure of great solidity — at once convent, fortress, and palace — built to last, not to change. In the long run, that construction becomes a confine, a prison. The United States was born of the Reformation and the Enlightenment. It came into being under the sign of criticism and self-criticism.[52]

The antagonistic notions about wealth creation in the two traditions added another aspect to the dichotomies: absolute versus limited government, non-existent property rights versus secure property rights, fiscal voracity versus fiscal limitations, and aversion to work versus self-realization through work.

The Censure of Usury

An example of the censure by the Catholic Church of activities that tended to generate profit is the case of usury, that is, charging a premium for lending money. This censure was based on an interpretation of the biblical principle of giving "without expecting anything in return." The initial prohibition against interest was sanctioned in the year 325 by the Council of Nicea and only applied to the clergy. The prohibition against "vile gain" was extended to laymen in Western Europe by Charlemagne's *Capitulares* and the Councils of the ninth century.[53]

In the early days of the subsistence economy, where barter and personal services were common, there were few opportunities for transactions that involved interest. But the prohibition on usury became more relevant with the gradual growth in trade and industry.

After the fall of Rome, the Church took on the features of an institution with a substantial increase in its spiritual and material power. By the Middle Ages, it had become one of the pillars of the existing economic structure. Its landholdings had increased so much that it was more powerful than the feudal barons, and its economic ideas were part of the moral teachings of Christianity.

Eric Roll writes that canonists accepted the Aristotelian distinction between the natural economy of the household and the anti-natural science of supply, that is, the art of earning money.[54] Aristotle's opposition to usury derived from his theory of the origin of money. Money, he wrote, arose as a medium to facilitate legitimate exchange, whose only purpose is to satisfy the needs of consumers. When Tertulian argued that eliminating greed would eliminate the reason for profit, and therefore, for commerce, the very foundations of commerce were being questioned. Saint Agustín feared that commerce would distract men from the search for God, and in the early Middle Ages the doctrine of *nullus christianus deber esse mercator* was common in the Church.[55]

During the Middle Ages, there were two responses to the development of trade and the growing opportunities for monetary transactions. On the one hand, the secular practice tended to encourage charging interest for money loans, justifying the practice in Roman Law. On the other, the Anglican Church, alarmed at these new developments, extended and made more strict its original prohibition.

The old prohibitions against interest were repeated in 1179 at the Council of Letran, under the papacy of Alexander III. "Given that the crime of usury is so prevalent everywhere that many have abandoned other business to become usurists, as if this occupation were legal, and in violation of both Testaments, we order that admitted usurists not be allowed to communion, and, should they die in sin, that they not be given Christian burial, and that no priest should accept their donations."[56]

Punishments for usury transcended religion, reaching even the legal sphere with annulment of wills, which usually were under the control of religious tribunals. This type of punishment was difficult to enforce since the majority of money lenders tended to be Jews, who had turned to moneylending because they were in those days generally marginalized from other types of industry and commerce for racial and religious reasons.[57]

Calvin, in 1574, denied that charging interest for the use of money was inherently sinful. He rejected Aristotle's notion of the sterility of money and maintained that it could be applied to activities that produced profit.

Open Institutions and Institutional Evolution

The British experience shows that the existence of open systems allows, through a process of trial and error, the discovery of new and better solutions to institutional challenges. On the other hand, closed systems tend to preclude such discoveries. It is not a coincidence that most of the financial and commercial institutions that still exist today had their origin in England and Holland in the Middle Ages.

Jorge Bustamante, in *Desregulación. Entre el derecho y la economía*, explains that for centuries mankind has attempted to improve the quality of life by increasing productivity and reducing costs—including transaction costs—through the development of new institutions that enable wealth creation and the movement of goods based on voluntary exchange. The most graphic example of this was the development of money, which meant that the limitations of bartering could be overcome and exchanges multiplied. Also contributing to the reduction of transaction costs were institutions such as bills of exchange, which allowed payments to be made in different markets without transferring cash; limited responsibility, which facilitates risking capital; shares of stock, which give liquidity to that capital; insurance, which allows risk to be spread more widely or be transferred to those who are less averse to risk (speculators); term markets; checks; credit cards; and so many others.[58]

The history of long-distance trade in the early days of modern Europe reveals an increasingly complex organization that eventually led to the boom of Western civilization. Transaction costs were reduced through organizational innovations and instruments, with specific techniques and enforcement characteristics, at three cost margins: 1) some increased capital mobility, 2) some reduced information costs, and 3) some spread risk.[59]

The origins of these innovations date back to ancient times; some evolved in the hands of the Medieval Italian city-states, Islam or Byzance. North comments that "among innovations that affected the mobility of capital were the techniques and methods evolved to evade usury law. The variety of ingenious ways by which interest was disguised in loan contracts ranged from 'penalties for late payment' to 'exchange rate manipulation,' to the early form of the mortgage; but all increased the cost of contracting. The costliness of usury laws was not only that they made the writing of contracts to disguise interest complex and cumbersome; but also that the enforceability of such contracts had become more problematic. As usury laws gradually broke down and higher rates of interest were permitted, the costs of writing contracts and the costs of enforcing them declined."[60]

The evolution of the bill of exchange, and especially the perfection of techniques and tools that increased its negotiability and the development of discounting methods, also affected the mobility of capital. In turn, these developments relied on the creation of institutions that encouraged their extended use and the growth of centers, like the fair at Champagne, and later banks and financial houses that specialized in discounting.

Another event that contributed to the reduction of transaction costs was the printing of prices of various commodities as well as the printing of manuals that provided information on weights, measures, uses, brokerage fees, postal systems, and in particular, the complex exchange rates among the European currencies and the world of trade. These innovations were the result of an increase in international trade volumes and, as such, were the consequence of economies of scale.

North writes that the "the final innovation was the transformation of uncertainty into risk." By uncertainty he refers to "a condition wherein one cannot ascertain the probability of an event and therefore cannot arrive at a way of insuring against such an occurrence. Risk, on the other hand implies the ability to make an actuarial determination of the likelihood of an event and hence insure against such an outcome. For example, marine insurance evolved from sporadic individual contracts covering partial payments for losses to contracts issued by specialized firms." On this subject, De Roover reports that marine insurance policies were codified by the fifteenth century. Printed forms were available in the sixteenth century that contained blank spaces for the particulars of each contract.[61]

North argues that specific innovations and particular institutional instruments evolved as a result of the reciprocal interplay of two basic economic forces. One was the economies of scale associated with the growing volume of trade; the other was the development of improved mechanisms for enforcing contracts at lower costs.

The development of enforcement mechanisms appears to have begun with the creation of internal codes of conduct in fraternal orders of guild merchants. Those who did not live up to them were threatened with ostracism. Merchants carried with them in long-distance trade codes of conduct, "so that Pisan laws passed into the sea codes of Marseilles ... Lubeck gave laws for the north of Europe ... and from Italy came the legal principle of insurance and bills of exchange."[62]

3

Public Conquest, Private Colonization

> *While North America was being populated by the more laborious and pure people of the most laborious nation in Europe, Spanish America was being populated with noblemen, military men and monks, who brought with them their tradition of public employment in government and the church. The idle nobility did not work, they made the enslaved and defeated natives work. In this way, they benefited doubly, by becoming rich with the work of others, and by degrading work so that the laborers would not become rich, and therefore prosperous and free.* —Juan B. Alberdi[63]

The colonization of Spanish America began with the voyage of discovery of 1492. From the beginning, the main objectives of the Spanish Crown were the pursuit of gold and silver to fill its coffers and spreading Christianity to the New World.

Spain was mostly a warring nation, the product of eight centuries of fighting with the Moors. War and maintaining the faith were the main objectives during those long eight centuries. García Hamilton wrote that the task of evangelizing the colonies was less authentic because the religion that was brought over to America was official and mandatory under the religious and territorial unification of Spain in 1492 with the conquest of Granada. One of the consequences of the religious "monopoly" can be appreciated in the writings of Hernán Cortés on the conquest of Mexico, which describe the destruction of the Aztec temples as one of the first things the Spaniards would do upon occupying a village.[64]

Juan B. Alberdi, a fierce critic of Spanish intentions in America, commented on how the American colonies adopted the features of its metropolis:

> From the beginning, Spanish America was warlike; it was neither industrial, commercial nor agricultural. It was badly populated, by a nation itself depopulated by eight centuries of wars. Its organic heritage was ignorance and a disdain for work; hatred for any dissident faith; love for the acquisition of gold without working; the misconception that having mines meant being rich, as long as one had slaves to work them; the error that extending the domains of the Crown meant extending its power and greatness; the hatred of any foreigner with different religion, commerce and treatment; isolation as a principle of social existence and a guarantee of security against being foreign; the prohibition against commerce ... the love for feasts, vices and luxury, the predilection for the mountainous countries of Mexico, New Granada, Quito, and Peru as rich in mines and natives capable of working for their idle masters ... the abandonment of the agricultural lands in South America, the distrust of work as a source of wealth, and the wealth of the country as the reason for independence and freedom....[65]

The Spanish traditions, according to Alberdi, became the forced heritage of Spanish America. Formal institutions, that is, codes, laws and regulations, were copied from the early Spanish statutes. But also the habits, uses, and even the way of thinking were legacies of Spain. Formal and informal institutions traveled the new continent with the *conquistadores*.

Mining

The pursuit of colonial objectives established mining as the primary activity, favored over farming and industry. Interestingly, mountainous mining areas of Latin America were developed earlier than rich, farming lands. Spain was not a farming nation, as the war had eliminated any incentive to develop sedentary and permanent activities. Cultivation of large parcels of land was very risky in times of armed conflicts. Continuous territorial disputes had reduced interest in farming to subsistence levels.

In America, mines in Potosí, Mexico (New Spain), Quito, New Granada, and Alto Peru grew in importance in the eyes of the Crown, over the Viceroyalty of the Río de la Plata, which had no mining potential. From the early royal provisions, the mines were property of the king, who granted concessions to individuals for exploitation. This notion later extended to the legislatures in Latin America: the institution of private property was not a priority since the work in mines did not require it.

In addition to being rich in minerals, these regions were populated with indigenous natives, whom they found useful to perform the mining tasks. In this sense, Spain colonized without colonists. No large contingents of workers arrived on the shores. The colonists were more like feudal barons who directed the work of the American Indians. Because the labor force was not Spanish, the colonists created institutions to organize the natives' work toward the colonists' goals. Mining being the main effort, the natives had to be organized to work in silver and gold mines.

To be developed, regions needed both the mining riches and the labor force to work in the mines; areas that had one or the other resource did not develop or they did so more slowly. Such was the case with Buenos Aires, which had neither and had to rely for growth on trade and smuggling.

The Religious Conquest

The Crown had well-defined public objectives. Economically, it sought a source of financing for the heavy governmental structure, the costs involved in maintaining the largest armada in the world, and the expenses of frequent wars, especially past debts incurred during the war against the Moors. In terms of territorial expansion, the colonization meant an increase in the Crown's power. In fact, it made Spain the most powerful empire in the world. In religious terms, colonization was an instrument for spreading Christianity. The Queen expressly wrote into the Royal Cedulas the duty of the *conquistador* to teach the Indians the Catholic faith. The establishment of religious congregation was one of the pillars of the Spanish settlements in America.

By the Papal Bulls of May 3 and 4, 1493, Pope Alexander VI donated to the Crown of Castile all lands "discovered or yet to be discovered" in the Indies with the stated purpose that those lands, their settlers, and inhabitants be converted to the Catholic faith. This purpose would be taken to heart by the Catholic monarchs and their successors and would be the supreme guideline for any and all plans for the economic development of the Indies.

> Despite the insistence of the Catholic Kings in innumerable instructions, orders, royal seals, and provisions which led to the voluminous Recollections of the Laws of Indies, what is certain is that the deficiencies of the missionary enterprise in the Americas were evident from the very beginning. Though the extremes reached by other imperial power, such as the systematic extermination of the native population, were not practiced by Spain, the quest for gold and the weakness in controlling the increasing alienation from the mother country resulted in unacceptable behavior, as much among the colonists as among the agents of the administration and even at times among the representatives of the Church delegates in the Indies.[66]

The conquest of Latin America was essentially a public initiative in which the unity of Church and State was at its highest point. Historian Alberto M. Salas wrote that, judged by its extraordinary legislation, the Spanish conquest acknowledges the religious finality of extending the Faith to the newly discovered world:

> Legal scholars prepared long requirements that had to be read to the Indians before taking any other action; these included brief descriptions of the principles of the Christian faith, the authority of the Pope, and the donation he had made to the Kings of Spain for their conversion. If the Indians refused to listen to this peaceful enunciation, the *conquistador* had the right to resort to arms and reduce them to obedience.[67]
>
> Those two cultures could not coexist peacefully and in equilibrium, because the *conquistador*, in addition to carrying out the imperial objective of spreading the beliefs, burning temples and gods, taking the gold and women he needed, using the Indians for farming and dividing them into *encomiendas* as a reward for services rendered to the Crown, noticed, from the very beginning, that the natives did not have weapons to defend the bountiful gifts that God had given them.[68]

Conquistador Hernán Cortés himself wrote about his religious purpose:

> We were moreover obligated as good Christians to pummel the enemies of our faith and by so doing, in the next world we win glory, and in this world we won more honor than any generation before us.[69]

García Hamilton wrote that the fact that the *conquistadores* did not have their families with them also affected the efficacy of the teachings. The Spaniards made the voyage from the Peninsula alone, and in America many of them consorted with Indian women and fathered their children. For the conquest of Mexico, Cortés had 550 men, 9 white women, and 16 horses. He settled down with Malinche and fathered children with several native women. Later on, after receiving the title of Marquis of the Valley of Oaxaca, he married Juana de Zúñiga. In Tabasco, the natives presented him with 20 young women in a gesture of peace and friendship, and in Tlaxcala, the military chiefs offered him their own daughters and he proceeded to distribute them among his captains.[70]

The Reaction of the Catholic Church to Unjust Labor Institutions

The most common labor systems were *encomienda*, *mita*, and *yanaconazgo*. La *encomienda* (also known as *repartimiento*) was a Spanish frontier institution transferred to America with the purpose of using indigenous labor and converting the natives to the Christian faith. An *encomienda* consisted of a group of Indians (linked by belonging to the same village or family) given to one of the Spanish *conquistadors* (*encomenderos*). The Indians were required to pay the *encomendero* a tribute in return for protection, religious instruction, and administration of justice. The tribute varied from region to region. In Alto Peru, for example, it was paid in gold and silver, while in Paraguay and Tucumán it was paid in workdays or in kind.[71]

In addition, the *encomendero* generally had a license to carry out some commercial activity, like hunting for wild horses or farming. In some regions, the *encomienda* system was used for the primitive manufactures such as cotton, wool, and leather.

Another institution that governed labor in Spanish America was the *mita*, which acquired special relevance during the exploitation of the mines in Potosí. *Mita* was an Inca institution that meant "shift," and under it the Indians were to spend long "shifts" of time laboring in the mines. In 1592, at the height of exploration in Potosí, there were between 13,000 and 17,000 *mitayos*. The Incas had utilized the system of the *mita* for construction, while the Spanish settlers used it for mining in Alto Peru and for certain farming and textile activities in Tucumán. The Jesuits and Franciscans complained vehemently about the harsh treatment of the *mitayos*.

Finally, *yanaconazgo* was similar to the *encomienda* system, but in this case the Indians were not related to each other, and in general it applied to groups of Indians who had lost their tribal connections due to war or illness.

Spanish ordinances abounded regarding the rules that governed the treatment of the natives by the colonists. The documents attempted to prevent abuses and the sale of natives, to regulate women's work, and to encourage conversion to Christianity.

With the gradual decline of the native population due to illnesses, forced migrations (the natives in Cuyo were taken from their homes to work in *mitas* in Alto Peru and Chile), changes in food habits, and the hardships of labor, etc., other institutions arose to organize native work. The *haciendas* became a kind of limited *encomienda*, with lower numbers of natives devoted almost exclusively to planting wheat and corn. The *encomenderos* became *hacendados*.

Increasing exploitation and inhuman treatment prevailed in America—despite the constant warnings by the Spanish monarchs. In 1511 the Dominican Fray Antonio de Montesinos made a vigorous protest against the exploitation of the natives. Historian Oreste Popescu observes,

"Horrified by the daily acts of barbarity of his compatriots, Montesinos invited the upper crust of the colony of La Española to mass in the Cathedral of Santo Domingo, on which occasion he preached the historic sermon, written with the intention of horrifying the colonists."[72] It is worth transcribing from Popescu the homily text:

> By what authority have you carried out such horrible wars against these people who were meek and peaceful in their lands, where such an infinite number of them, by death or havoc never before heard of, you have consumed them? How can you keep them so oppressed and exhausted, without giving them food or healing them of their illnesses, that they incur from the excessive work you put upon them and they die for you, or better said, you kill them in order to remove and acquire gold every day?... Be sure that in the state in which you are, you cannot save your soul more than the Moors and Turks who do not share or want our Holy faith.[73]

Montesinos's words spread around the colony and soon made their way to Spain. His efforts were reflected in the Laws of Burgos passed in December 1512, the first code of social legislation in the Indies.[74]

The Laws of Burgos, although accepting the system of *encomienda* as just given the natives' "natural inclination to idleness and vices," prohibited the *encomenderos* from mistreating the workers, protected them from being hit, incarcerated, insulted, or used as beasts of burden, and exempted pregnant women from work, etc. The Laws also obliged the *encomenderos* to guarantee humane working conditions, build adequate housing, grant rest, feed and clothe the Indians properly, and teach them in schools and churches. Moreover, they were supposed to teach those with higher abilities to read and write, and for the sons of chiefs, older than thirteen, four years of instruction were mandatory. According to Popescu, these educational measures were the starting point for the creation of teaching centers for the Indians founded and run by the Franciscan priests.

Fray Montesinos devoted his life to fighting with the Crown to humanize the treatment of the indigenous people. His most fervent disciple was an *encomendero* who had land and mining business dealings with the Indians in Española and Cuba. In 1514, Bartolomé de Las Casas "decided to abandon his successful business, he gave up the Indians he had under *encomienda* and joined the ranks of the defenders of the Indians for the rest of his life." He prepared a bill to end the *encomiendas* and replace the system with one that was compatible with the goal of converting the native population:

> Completely convinced that the *encomienda* system had transformed itself into an instrument of enslavement and exploitation of natives, Las Casas

in 1515 sailed to Spain together with Montesinos to begin the battle of his life for the abolition of the *encomiendas* and for their substitution by an economic system compatible with the goals of evangelizing the natives. Beginning from this moment, he would elaborate an entire series of projects which he presented to the royal court, accompanied with calculations of cost and sometimes including the incomes which would enter the royal treasury, if his plans were put into action.[75]

In 1518, the Crown granted him a concession to colonize Christian laborers, who were awarded tax exemptions, grains, tools, animals, and other benefits. But, in the end, Las Casas' plan failed. The greed of the *conquistadores* and the extraordinary lure of the Peruvian gold mines were too much for the noblemen and the laborers he had brought over. Oreste Popescu reports that Las Casas joined the Order of Preachers and entered a monastery. Many years later, Juan Bautista Alberdi would take up the cause.[76]

The Administration of the New Continent

Octavio Paz wrote that the new Spanish domains were never formally colonies, in the traditional sense of the word. New Spain and Peru were Viceroyalties, kingdoms under the Crown of Castile, like other Spanish kingdoms. In contrast, the English settlements in New England and other areas were colonies in the classic sense of the term, that is, communities established in foreign territory, that preserved their cultural, religious, and political bond with the motherland.[77]

The economic history of Spanish America perpetuated the centralized and bureaucratic traditions from its heritage. John Coatsworth wrote about the institutions of Mexico in the nineteenth century that every economic enterprise operated in the political sphere. Larger operations relied on connections to local and colonial officials to facilitate virtually every aspect of business activity. Smaller ventures operated at the margins of the law; they existed only at the mercy of local powers and never with any protection from greater powers.[78]

Early on, those who exercised power in America were in fact the *adelantados*, who had been granted concessions by the Crown to explore new lands and claim them in the name of the king, to look for a route to East India, to spread Christianity, and pay tribute to Spain. An *adelantado* had the triple role of governor enforcing the laws of Spain and its public administration; captain general leading the expedition troops; and chief justice, because he heard judicial matters.[79]

The *adelantado* was an institution from the Peninsula whose origins lay in the war against the Moors. Originally, he was an *adelantado de frontera*, a nobility title that the king awarded the military chief of the border castle or town whose main role was the defense of the border against the enemy. The *adelantado* had *de facto* public power because he was in a situation of permanent conflict.

Historian David Rock has described the rituals and customs associated with the founding of cities. City locations depended on the availability of Indians and the potential for successful farming. Once a location was chosen, authorities would issue a proclamation regarding the city's creation, choose officeholders for the *cabildo,* and establish the Church. Residents were divided into the white *vecinos* and the *moradores,* who were usually non-white.[80]

The Cabildos

The *cabildos* were the basic unit of political, judicial, economic, and social administration in the Spanish colonies in America. Following the medieval practice in Spain, at first *cabildo* officials were elected. But later, from about 1610 onward, offices were put up for sale, and they fell into the hands of local settler oligarchies.[81] The responsibilities of the *cabildos* show the extent of public intervention in the commercial and civil matters of the colonies. Among them were the regulation of food prices, supplies and wage rates; they supervised political administration, exercised police and defense functions, regulated the supply of food, administered weights and measures, distributed lands and controlled transfers of title, collected municipal taxes, declared holidays and planned public festivities, administered criminal and civil justice, maintained jails and roads, inspected hospitals, provided for the welfare of the poor and orphans, and in general attended to citizens' needs. *Cabildos* also represented the settlers in their disputes with the Crown, regulated occupations and rural and urban industries.[82] In addition, the *cabildos* were in charge of granting commercial licenses, permits, and other rights.

The Monopoly of Trade

The goal of the Spanish Crown to secure as much precious metal as possible was achieved in two ways: first, through levies imposed on commercial activities in the colonies, and second, through commercial exchanges.[83] In pursuit of this goal, the Crown devised a complex trade regime between the colonies and the mainland that tended to raise import duties for the former, while the costs of production were lowered by the use of slave labor of natives in the mines. With production costs lowered, income could be directed toward importing industrial goods from Spain.

Trade was monopolized to ensure the flow of precious metals from the colonies to Europe. From 1503 until 1717, most of the trade to and from the colonies had to go through Seville, while in America, the only authorized ports were Veracruz (Mexico) and Portobello (in what is today Panama). Spanish merchandise destined for Mexico had to go through Veracruz, while Portobello was the port for the rest of the Spanish colonies.

The boom in piracy in the sixteenth century made the Spanish government pass stricter trade regulations and to implement a system of convoys that annually sailed to the Antilles; from there, those going to Portobello turned to their destination in order to trade wine, olives, iron, mercury, fabrics, and luxury items for gold, silver, leather, and some medicinal spices from Peru. The rest of the ships went to Veracruz to exchange with the colonies in New Spain (Mexico).

In addition to the monopoly that the system of convoys created, there were other regulations and levies on trade. Historian Harold U. Faulkner recounts how quicksilver, tobacco, salt and gunpower monopolies, as well as excises and duties on other goods, restricted trade. Cultivation of hemp, tobacco, olives, and vineyards was prohibited in the colonies, and the king drew a 20 percent royalty from the mining of silver and gold.[84]

> Statutory restrictions, the ban against trade among colonies and with other nations, and the monopolistic systems of galleons and fleets, in addition to other restrictions on trade — all contributed to the inevitable smuggling, undertaken not only by England and Holland but by private companies. One private company, the Dutch East India Company, would eventually command a veritable naval fleet.[85] Smuggling and the loss of supremacy at sea — which would occur in the seventeenth century after the defeat of the Invincible Armada — marked the beginning of the decline of the Spanish Empire in America and the rise of new powers, especially France, Portugal, and England.

To counter the expansion of smuggling, a very strict set of statutes was enacted, which multiplied customs inspections and other onerous rules. The cost of the system fell on legal trade, making the fiscal burden even heavier and stimulating the very activity it aimed to curtail.

America: Hope for the Miserable and Persecuted

The British Crown neither financed nor supported the attempts at colonizing North America. From the beginning, expeditions were financed and arranged by private individuals and groups.

> As in the case of New France and New Netherlands, the first colonization by the English was carried on by private corporations, chartered by the government, a type of trading company which had been developing for a half century prior to the Jamestown experiment. The English crown was unwilling to incur the trouble and expense of founding colonies, but it was glad to grant charters to corporations or individuals who were inclined to risk their own fortunes in such attempts. The expense and difficulties encountered in transporting colonists, equipping them with agricultural appliances, and keeping them alive until the first crops were harvested were so great that only the expectation of future grain and the grant of the broadest powers in the charters could entice stockholders to invest their money in colonizing companies.[86]

The first charter, granted to John Cabot in 1496, was financed by merchants from Bristol and London and included monopoly rights to commerce as well as the obligation to turn over to the Crown one-fifth of the wealth found in the New World.

It was not until a century later that the British monarch paid any attention to voyages to America. Queen Elizabeth I granted Sir Humphrey Gilbert the right to "inhabit and hold all the remote and pagan lands that did not belong to any Christian prince" in exchange for one-fifth of the gold and silver that were found. The expeditions by Gilbert, and later by his half-brother, Sir Walter Raleigh, were difficult, and the small colonies they founded in Terranova and Virginia disappeared soon thereafter. Though losing their personal fortunes in the attempts, they set the tone for the English colonization of North America. Historian Jorge Cárdenas Nannetti writes about the relevance of these expeditions:

> In a period of 15 years, Raleigh organized and financed at least six attempts of colonization, from Terranova to Florida, although he did not accompany them personally, by express royal prohibition. One of the early ones was under the command of his step-brother, Sir Humphrey Gilbert, to whose colonists the Queen granted in writing "all the privileges of free citizens and naturals of England, as broad as if they had been born and resided personally in our kingdom." This acknowledgment was politically very important in the subsequent struggle between democracy and absolutism.[87]

The failure of individual attempts gave way to an institution that is a landmark of capitalist Europe: the joint stock company. By royal order of 1606, the London Company and the Plymouth Company were organized, and they quickly proceeded to assemble fleets destined for the Atlantic coast of North America. These companies had absolute ownership rights to natural riches and to impose limited export and import duties. In exchange, they agreed to colonize the territory and to pay one-fifth of the gold and silver found.

Interesting mechanisms were used to finance the companies: they sold shares in the corporation to finance the voyage and gave away shares and free trips to volunteer colonists. To pay for the shares or the voyage, some colonists entered into a sort of voluntary slavery, became "white indentured servants," as they were known. Many who wanted to emigrate to the New World sold their freedom for a period of three to seven years to one of the companies in exchange for the voyage over and a parcel of land in America. (The cost of the fare equaled seven years' income of a laborer in England. The period of the contracts depended on how much the colonist contributed in money or in kind.) When that period expired, the colonist recovered his freedom and acquired ownership rights to his land.

The early companies failed shortly after beginning the colonization. The Plymouth Company was absorbed in 1629 by the Massachusetts Bay Company, whose shareholders were mostly Puritan merchants. The colonists in Virginia bought the interests of the London Company.

In the period 1629–30, the English government adopted a tyrannical attitude toward religious dissidents. This gave a distinctive flavor to the immigration toward America, since the Puritan leaders saw in Massachusetts an ideal refuge against religious persecution.[88]

Many well off and qualified merchants who did not want to emigrate as servants bought shares in the company and agreed to observe the precepts of the royal charter. Faulkner writes that "the Massachusetts Bay was colonized by the very managers of the Company and in its early years, its government was notably similar to a modern corporation. Free men were shareholders and the governor, lieutenant governor and the eighteen members of the government were figures comparable to the president, vice-president and a board of directors of a corporation."

Nor were the establishments that succeeded those in Plymouth and Virginia initiated by the Crown. The English kings did not participate in the colonization efforts, except through collecting taxes and establishing some minor regulations. Colonization ventures after those of the London and Plymouth Companies were organized exclusively by groups of emigrants from the colonies and by wealthy landowners.

Rhode Island was established by a religious division in Massachusetts. Puritanism in Massachusetts was extreme, and dissidents were persecuted and punished. Roger Williams was expelled from Salem for religious reasons. In 1636, Williams purchased lands from the natives, founded Providence, and gave it a constitution that guaranteed religious freedom.

> In Williams' thinking, the new government rested on popular sovereignty, liberty, equality, and, as a check to excessive power, frequent elections were established, as well as a single-chamber legislature, individual or collective initiative for statutes, referendums, and the right to derogate any statute by vote. "Man can live as his conscience dictates," read a provision approved in 1646. Rhode Island became a refuge for Quakers and for all religious and political dissidents.[89]

Connecticut also split off from Massachusetts, when some farmers wanted to have access to better lands and to trade with the natives. They built cabins and later founded villages, giving themselves their own constitutions and government. Maine and New Hampshire were colonized by English emigrants protected by Sir Ferdinand Gorges and Captain John Mason, who received the royal charter for colonization. Dissidents from Massachusetts also inhabited those areas.

According to English law, neither the settlers in Rhode Island nor those in Connecticut had legal title to those lands. They were mere "intruders in the domains of the king,"[90] but eventually were granted royal recognition.

To the South, the colonies were founded by individual initiatives through royal concessions and contracts that gave the founders a sort of feudal status, with all the associated rights and attributions. Yet, in many cases the Crown included restrictive clauses stating that the laws should be established with and by the consent of freemen.

In fact, the colonies needed people and had to attract them with favorable conditions that were not the rule in England or in other colonies. Colonists had to be wooed with institutions such as religious freedom, private property, civil liberties, and representative government.

William Penn, a Quaker leader, founded the colony of Pennsylvania, with Philadelphia as its first city, and enacted a constitution based on religious respect, representative government, equality under the law, and a government that was limited to legislate on punishment for violating the law. The colony issued prospectuses in German and Dutch to attract settlers. Thousands of Quakers from Europe eventually arrived, and Philadelphia quickly became the premier city in the New World.

Maryland was founded by Cecil Calvers as a refuge for Catholics, who in those days were intensely persecuted by English puritans. New York was the property of the Duke of York, despite a brief Dutch occupation. New Jersey was founded by George Carteret and Sir John Berkeley. The colony of Georgia was founded in a philanthropic effort in 1733 by General James Oglethorpe, a member of the British Parliamentary commission investigating the conditions of English prisons. Oglethorpe had intended to found a colony for the rehabilitation of convicts, debtors, and others persecuted in England.

The Carolinas were founded by farmers attempting to occupy fertile lands to the South of Virginia. These landowners had the right to appoint judges and governors, attract colonists, give lands, and manage the colony. Limits were established by the concessions granted by the Crown, and especially, by the colonists themselves. In order to attract colonists, they had to offer institutional systems that were relatively convenient; and they had no authority beyond those granted by the royal charter and by the colonists themselves.

North American colonists came to develop their own lives. They had no purposes of participation in public life. Only the concession holders had to fulfill certain objectives of the Crown, not the common colonists. America was the land where they would realize the dreams and projects they could not achieve in England, and so, the New World became the hope for the humble and the persecuted. It was not the powerful landowners that emigrated, but the poor, many of whom sold their freedom to pay for the voyage.

The objectives they pursued were economic insofar as they sought to escape the scarcity they had suffered in England, but they also intended to live freely by their religious beliefs. They brought with them informal English institutions. The limitation of power, participation in public matters through elections or meetings, resistance to abuse of power — all these values they transplanted to America. The same was true for religious beliefs. Most of the religious denominations condemned idleness, waste, and debt. In the colonies, violators suffered physical punishment and incarceration.

In general, the settlers were farmers, artisans, sailors, or manufacturers. They came to America with the intention to live on the income from their respective occupations. Toward 1754, 90 percent of the 1.3 million inhabitants of the English colonies were farmers. In times of peace, relations with the natives were commercial. Wars arose over territorial disputes. There were no serious attempts by the settlers to convert the natives or to make them work in their enterprises.

For Spain, the conquest of America was a modern version of the crusades, aimed at creating a universal Christian empire and deriving income for the Crown. In English America, colonization was a private endeavor, and its central purpose was to find an environment in which people could be free from the religious persecution suffered in Great Britain.

The contrast between the two processes is striking: public conquest versus private colonization; imposition of a single faith versus religious freedom; immigration of military men, noblemen, priests, and bureaucrats versus immigration of those devoted to agriculture and commerce; predominantly male immigration versus immigration of entire families; centralized administration versus autonomy of the colonies; and strong presence of the Crown in pursuit of mining rent versus low government participation.

4
Post-Independence Institutional Continuity in America

> *The plant of civilization is not grown from seed, but propagated from the vine.* — Juan B. Alberdi

The early part of the nineteenth century was characterized by shifts in balance of power. Spain's continued decline reached its lowest point during Napoleon's invasion to the Peninsula, which had been preceded by the defeat to the British in the Seven Years War (1763). The activities of local groups in the Spanish colonies were inspired by the success of the Revolutions both in the United States in 1776 and France in 1789. At the same time, England was becoming more interested in selling its increased manufacturing output, and colonies in America attempted to overcome the restrictive trade regime imposed by the Crown.

The revolutions that gave birth to the present countries in Latin America were the result of many decades of pent-up pressure. Spain succumbed to Napoleon in 1807, and the colonies could no longer tolerate the Spanish trade monopoly and isolation.

John Lynch writes that at the time of the collapse of Spain, the country ruled a vast empire with 7 million subjects, divided into four Viceroyalties and extending from California to Cape Horn, from the mouth of the Orinoco River to the Pacific Coast. Fifteen years later, the empire's holdings had been reduced to Cuba and Puerto Rico. Independence for the colonies was precipitated by an external shock, but in fact they had already been developing their own identities.[91] For decades after independence, bloody struggles occurred among local groups to consolidate independence from Spain and to decide who would succeed the Spaniards, with each country resolving the troubles in its own way.

Following independence, the new Latin American nations attempted to organize themselves on the federal principles of the United States. Whereas in the latter case, autonomous colonies delegated specific functions to the national government, centralism had been the rule for Latin American institutions — from the absolutist Spain that attempted to consolidate the fusion of the kingdoms of Castile and Aragon, to the administration of the colonies of the New World by the viceroys, which was described by historian Carlos Floria as the "arms of the king."

Trade, Monopoly and Independence

Toward the end of the eighteenth century, at the early signs of crisis, the Spanish Bourbons developed strategies aimed at retaining the colonies. But the unexpected result of these administrative reforms was to strengthen the colonies' regional identity. Moreover, one aspect of the reform — appointing Spaniards to administrative posts to replace locals — focused more attention on imperial control. In 1739, the Viceroyalty of Nueva Granada — which included Venezuela, Colombia, Panama, and Ecuador — was separated from Peru. In order to strengthen competition against Portugal-Brazil, the Viceroyalty of the Río de la Plata was established in 1776, and the province of Charcas (now Bolivia) was separated from Lima's administrative control and placed under the jurisdiction of Buenos Aires. In Havana, Caracas, and Santiago de Chile new Captainships were established and awarded considerably more autonomy from the Viceroyalties. Here and there, *criollos* were appointed to high posts, but control of the bureaucracy remained firmly in Spanish hands. The increased controls limited the ability of *criollos* to evade royal oppression. John Lynch wrote that "public office could be bought, fiscal obligations were negotiable and restrictions to commerce were ignored."[92]

These measures increased the costs to the *criollos* of putting up with the status quo, generating more incentives toward change. Smuggling — the market response to the restrictive trade policies of the Crown — allowed *criollos* to quantify just how bad the situation had become. England, anxious to sell products, became the natural ally of emerging nations in their struggle for change.

The monopolistic trade regime that Spain imposed on the colonies could not be sustained. As inequities, product shortages, and high prices became more flagrant, the colonies expanded economic relations among

4. Post-Independence Institutional Continuity in America

themselves, and trade among the colonies developed independently of the transatlantic system.[93]

England's dual strategic goal was to obtain markets for its output and at the same time dominate American trade routes that would strengthen its position. Until 1815, when the local markets were overabundant, England deposited in Latin America its surplus industrial production.

> But England's role proved to be essential in supporting the former colonies during Spain's attempts at recovering them after 1815. In the following decade, England was very pleased to consolidate relations with the new nations through trade, navigation, and friendship treaties. In those days, England's power was predicated upon its commercial and naval power and on the strength of its international treaties.

In the period following independence, throughout Latin America, from Mexico to Buenos Aires, the richest, most prestigious portion of local trade remained in foreign hands. Fifty years after arriving in Buenos Aires or Valparaiso, English family names abounded among local aristocracy. The Liverpool route replaced that of Cadiz.[94]

According to Halperín, in many respects England was Spain's heir and the beneficiary of a monopolistic situation that can be defined more in economic than legal terms. While Spain dominated regional commerce by imposing legal restrictions to competition, England did it through competition, or at least within the guidelines of commercial treaties. He goes on to add that the Hispanic America that emerged in 1825 was different from its incarnation around 1810. With the expansion of transatlantic commerce, it learned to consume more, and foreign goods started to replace local artisan products:

> Those *serapes* made in Glasgow to the Mexican taste, which can be bought in Saltillo for less than those made in Saltillo; those *ponchos* made in Manchester as if they had been made in the *pampa*, bad but inexpensive; the Toledan knives made in Sheffield; ordinary cotton wool made in New England, which more than the British one, triumphs over that made in the Andes.[95]

This policy of greater commercial openness by the recently established governments in Latin America became an important source of fiscal revenues. Halperín Donghi writes that a policy of banning imports would not only have been unpopular but would also have deprived the new states of custom duties, which, due to pressure from landowners, tended to fall on imports and constituted the largest portion of public revenues.

Before the major investments in the second half of the nineteenth century, Hispanic America appears to have enjoyed a less visible type of foreign investment: some foreign businessmen translated a portion of their commercial gains into the purchase of local lands.[96]

Independence Wars, Militarization and Stagnation

The social consequences of the hard-fought independence wars were important, while the economic ones, except in a few isolated areas, were truly disastrous. But the most relevant and obvious of these consequences was the militarization of the emerging republics. In his book *The Centralist Tradition of Latin America*, Claudio Véliz explains in the chapter on "The Survival of Political Centralism" how the subordinate role of the military during colonial rule was transformed. As civilian armies were formed and officers chosen, the military became a ready route for social advancement. Typically, after the war, generals became landowners, wielding both social and political power.[97]

After the chaos of independence wars, the republics underwent periods of disorder and anarchy under authoritarian regimes that represented *sui generis* versions of Iberian centralism. There are enough factors to explain this development. The ideas of leaders like San Martín, O'Higgins, Santa Cruz, Bolívar, and Sucre were more aligned with the paternalism of Spanish enlightenment than with any form of Western Europe's liberalism. The regimes led by these men "did not differ from frankly authoritarian governments and their behaviors were closer to early despotism than to an ideological revolution."[98]

José I. García Hamilton described the effect of the independence wars on reinforcing the militaristic traditions in Latin American societies:

> With the independence struggle from Spain, the war effort became once again the main task in American communities. Generals Simón Bolívar, José de San Martín, Antonio de Sucre, became the paradigms of our societies. Ricardo Rojas called San Martín "the Saint of the Sword" and Belisario Roldán bordered on idolatry when he included [San Martín] in his famous Civic Prayer: "Our Father who art in bronze."

In *El crimen de la guerra*, Juan Bautista Alberdi wrote that South America's only contribution to universal civilization had been its independence wars. He wrote that there was "no invention comparable to Franklin's lightning rod, Fulton's steamboat, or Morse's telegraph, all of which are North American. Not in the physical sciences, the achievements

4. Post-Independence Institutional Continuity in America 53

of industry, nor in any aspect of human knowledge does the world know a South American glory that can be recognized as such. The only glory that exists there is military glory; the only great men are great warriors. That is why every ruler wants to be a Bolívar, or aspires to be a San Martín."[99]

The decades that followed were characterized, on the one hand, by fragmentation and the struggle for avoiding re-conquest by Spain and, on the other, by the establishment of a new balance among the emerging Latin American political units. In 1816, the Provinces of the Río de la Plata declared their independence six years after having deposed the viceroy. In 1818, so did Chile, having also expelled its governor in 1810. At the north end of the empire, the conservative Mexicans opted for independence in 1821 and an empire ruled by Iturbide.

Violent battles and bloody retaliation marked the period 1810 to 1824, producing martyrs and heroes in the struggle against Spanish domination, from Bolivia to Venezuela. Later, Paraguay chose to secede from the Provinces of the Río de la Plata (now Argentina), and so eventually did Uruguay. In 1826, Bolivia became a separate entity, seceding from its allies Argentina and Peru. In 1823 the Mexicans deposed the recently named emperor, as the nascent Provinces of Central America seceded from Mexico. After a decade of revolts and *coups d'état*, in 1838 Guatemala, El Salvador, Honduras, Nicaragua, and Costa Rica raised their national flags. In 1830, the nucleus of Bolivar's vision of regional unity, Great Colombia (1821–1830), was divided into Venezuela, Colombia, and Ecuador.

Between 1830 and 1903, Uruguay had over 40 armed struggles, and the country participated in armed conflicts among its two large neighbors, as well as the 1864–1870 war, in which the alliance of Argentina, Brazil, and Uruguay defeated Paraguay, inflicting devastating losses of lives and territory. Bolivia had an even harder time: after winning one war (against Peru) and losing two (against Argentina and Chile), in the 126 years from independence until 1952 it suffered no less than 178 rebellions and uprisings. Mexico, whose political development was indelibly sealed by the Texas revolutionary war in 1830 and by a costly war against the United States in the 1840s, ranked first in presidential replacements. According to William Glade, Antonio L. de Santa Anna set a continental record for the number of times that he walked in and out of office.

As a result of the high number of changes of presidents and dictators, the second half of the 1800s represent the longest period of despotic rule of chiefs of state, among them Guzmán Blanco (1870–1888) and Gómez (1908–1935) in Venezuela; Barrios (1871–1885), Estrada Cabrera (1898–1920), and Ubico (1931–1944) in Guatemala; García Moreno (1860–1875) in Ecuador; Francia (1880–1840), C. A. López (1841–1862) and

F. S. López (1862–1870) in Paraguay; and Santos Zelaya (1893–1909) in Nicaragua.[100]

After the revolutions, a recurring source of conflict was the lack of consensus among the different regions on who would succeed the king. Monarchical legitimacy had imposed a high cost on dissidence, but with the revolutionary break with Spain, legitimacy vanished and attempts at autonomy, even secession, were easier. Permanent sources of revenue were necessary to consolidate the power of the state and maintain vital military forces in remote territories. Taxes had previously been levied on mining in Potosí and now shifted to taxes on trade, which were collected at the only maritime port, Buenos Aires. The revenue from the new duties was not sufficient to replace the old sources, and disputes ensued over who had the right to collect duties for the port of Buenos Aires.[101]

According to Roberto Cortés Conde, in Argentina, while the central state needed money to establish the army, landowners in the countryside resorted to cavalry, a cheaper alternative in areas with abundant pastures. They replaced the central state in the provision of public goods, maintaining some measure of order, albeit primitive and despotic. Quasi-private armies were formed with farm hands, horsemen, and cattle owned by the landowners. Strongmen, *caudillos*, exacted compensation in exchange for providing some public goods. And public finances became confused with those of the ruler.[102]

In times of uncertainty and war, military and administrative activities appeared more profitable than commercial enterprises. Halperín Donghi writes that the negative side of independence became very obvious: degradation of administration, disorder, militarization, and a despotism that is less acceptable because it is imposed on populations that have awakened to political life and whose only feared alternative is civil war. On the economic side, throughout Hispanic America, stagnation seemed insurmountable, with international trade levels in 1850 barely exceeding those of 1825.[103]

The constant armed struggles generated uncertainty in terms of private property rights and the prevailing rules. During the first half of the nineteenth century, neither England nor any other European country made substantial investments in Hispanic America. The decisions to abstain from such investments tended to be worded as censure to post-revolutionary order.[104] With the sole exception of the sugar plantations of the Atlantic, the new "owners of the market" were not interested in the fruits of agriculture and cattle. And although mining was a more enticing alternative, it did not generate capital investments necessary for sources of precious metals to regain their productivity.

4. Post-Independence Institutional Continuity in America

During the first half of the nineteenth century, the lack of limitation to government power in Argentina resulted in war. Later, a national agreement was reached on revenues: domestic customs were eliminated, and the provinces would share in national custom duties. The fight between centralists ("*unitarios*") and federalists ("*federales*") was in fact a fight for fiscal revenues. Integration to the world economy was a win-win situation from the domestic point of view and in terms of fiscal revenues. It also enabled the formation of a national army and the strengthening of the national state.

Not all the new Latin American countries had the ability to adjust to new economic circumstances, and the duration of post-independence wars varied from country to country. For instance, both Venezuela (whose independence wars happened repeatedly on its own territory) and the Provinces of the Río de la Plata (whose independence wars happened away from its own territory but which suffered long blockades and extended periods of disorder) managed to recover and exceed the levels of the most prosperous colonial days. Since before 1810, Venezuela in agriculture and the Río de la Plata in livestock both had the kernel of a transatlantic economic structure that to a certain degree would compensate for the political and social disadvantages resulting from their new commercial organization.

In the rest of Latin America the process was slower. The economies that had relied traditionally on mining, like Bolivia, Peru, and especially Mexico—deeply affected by the revolutionary crisis—did not go back to the economic levels of colonial times. Mexican silver production dropped to half. In 1810, while still Spanish territory, Mexico's exports had amounted to five times the value of those of the Río de la Plata, but by mid-century, they were equivalent. Even more striking is the fact that after only 40 years, the farm wealth of the pampa of the Río de la Plata—which prior to 1810 had exported amounts equal to 4 percent of Mexican silver exports—had almost equaled in value: the latter grew tenfold while the former were reduced to half.[105]

At the same time, in the central plateau of Costa Rica the expansion of coffee began. Owners became wealthy by reinvesting profits from previous harvests to plant increasingly more coffee. That tiny corner of Central America found—as had the provinces of the Río de la Plata and Venezuela—the "new formula for prosperity" in an export economy tied to transatlantic trade.

Together with the Río de la Plata, Venezuela, Chile, Costa Rica, and the Spanish Antilles enjoyed a good economic situation. Cuba expanded its sugar production, having benefited from the freedom of slaves from the English Antilles. Brazil also overcame its independence crisis without immediate economic difficulties. As in Cuba, the sugar crisis in the West Indies represented an immediate stimulus, and the Northeast returned to prosperity at the same time as the Río de la Plata expanded in the South of the continent.

In brief, the independence wars planted the seed of a militarist tradition in Latin America, assigning to military forces a lasting role in politics. Economically, the first half of the century was characterized by uncertainty, first arising out of the independence process, and later, from the fight to establish new political units.

Federalism in the United States

The successful experiment in the United States would become an inescapable model for organizing the new Latin American nations. As the second half of the eighteenth century began, the colonies were still autonomous. Years passed and tensions mounted between Britain and the colonies. In 1774 a Continental Congress was convened, with delegates from all colonies except Georgia. The main role of the Congress was to act as a counterpart to the English Parliament in its dealings with the colonies.

With the independence war under way by 1775-76, the Continental Congress advised the colonies to form new governments. A year after Independence was declared, the states—with the exceptions of Massachusetts, Connecticut, and Rhode Island—had passed new constitutions.

The interests and problems that the colonies had in common led them to draft constitutions and develop autonomous political institutions. Each new state designed its form of government independently from the others. James Madison wrote,

> Nothing has excited more admiration in the world than the manner in which free governments have been established in America; for it was the first instance from the creation of the world ... the free inhabitants have been seen deliberating on a form of government, and selecting such of their citizens as possessed their confidence, to determine upon and give effect to it.[106]

State constitutions shared three main features that distinguish them from those elsewhere. First, they were (in most cases) widely debated by the population; second, they reflected democratic ideals within limited government; and third, they represented an advance over institutions that had been in force during colonial times.

In some states constitutions were subjected to intense debates. In

Massachusetts, the first constitutional text was rejected; a constitutional assembly was convened and the text was submitted to the people for discussion in town meetings where individual sections were analyzed. This process took over five years, and the constitution was finally passed on June 15, 1780.[107] The constitutions of Maryland, Pennsylvania, and North Carolina were drafted by legislative bodies authorized and ratified by the people.

These constitutions included British institutions like the Bill of Rights. The constitution that George Mason drafted for Virginia listed fundamental liberties that already existed in British law such as "moderate bail and humane punishments, the establishment of a militia instead of a permanent army, quick judicial process regulated by the laws of the country, and judgment by peers, freedom of thought, freedom of the press, the right of the majority to reform or change government, and a ban against mass arrests."[108]

Other states "considerably augmented the list of institutions according to their own experience or documents like the British *Bill of Rights* of 1688." Among those added were "freedom of expression, of gathering, of petitioning authorities, the right to bear arms, the right to *habeas corpus*, the inviolability of the household, equality before the law, bans on retroactive laws, on taking private property without compensation, on jail without a warrant, on applying martial law in times of peace and on making somebody bear witness against oneself."[109]

The division of power among three branches (Legislative, Executive and Judicial) was also included in the state constitutions. The Executive power was to be an elective office and for definite terms, in contrast with Britain where the king inherited the throne.

In 1777, the Continental Congress of 1774 became the Congress of the Confederacy. States passed the Articles of Confederation and Perpetual Union establishing that each state would hold one vote, and that consensus of nine of the thirteen states was required for important decisions, such as declaring war, borrowing money, signing treaties, recruiting forces, and appointing a commander in chief. In turn, Congress could establish executive departments and proceeded to appoint foreign affairs, finance, war, and an admiralty commission and establish a post office.

The powers of Congress reflected the delegation made by the states to the Confederacy, but they resembled the functions that the king and Parliament held before independence.

> The Articles of Confederation sought to preserve the independence and sovereignty of the states. The Federal Government received only those

powers which the colonies had recognized as belonging to the king and parliament. Thus Congress was given all powers connected with war and peace, expect the important one of taxation to support a war. It could conclude no commercial treaty limiting the states' rights to collect custom duties. It had power to establish post offices and charge postage (the only taxing power it possessed) to set standards of weights and measures, and to coin money. These were sovereign powers which the king had exercised without question.[110]

The initial refusal of the states to acknowledge the legislature's fiscal power was the kernel of a later dispute among so-called "federalists" and "antifederalists." Only a year after achieving independence, the states were not ready to cede to the legislature what they had denied Parliament.

The initial proposal suggested a weak central power with enumerated and specific functions, whereas the states governed over all issues within the framework of the republican form of government, the bill of rights, and private property rights. States repeatedly aborted attempts to delegate taxing power on the Confederacy.

A few years later, in 1786, there was concern about possible dissolution of the Union due to the scarce power, functions, and resources of the Congress of the Confederation.

The trade restrictions imposed by Britain negatively affected the economy of the states most dependent on those transactions, like Virginia and Massachusetts. The issue of trade and attempts to restore relations with Britain became an incentive for the states to meet again. Alexander Hamilton and James Madison persuaded the delegates to convene a convention to reconstitute the federal government.

Thus started the key dispute between the federalists—supporters of a strong central government that would not encroach on the powers of the states—and antifederalists—who warned of the dangers of a powerful central state and its advance over individuals and liberty.

A representative quote follows from Antifederalist Paper No. 1:

> I had rather be a free citizen of the small republic of Massachusetts, than an oppressed subject of the great American empire.... If we can confederate upon terms that will secure to us our liberties, it is an object highly desirable.... but if it will endanger our liberties as it stands, let it be amended.[111]

After many months of heated debates, the federalists prevailed. But the efforts of the antifederalists were not fruitless. The new federal

4. Post-Independence Institutional Continuity in America 59

government would have fiscal and trade powers, but would not be exempt from limitations.

> Yet the Constitution is not a unitary one, for although the government it creates is supreme within its sphere, that sphere is defined and limited. As the Tenth Amendment made clear in 1791, "the powers not delegated to the United States by the Constitution, nor prohibited by it to the Stares, are reserved to the States respectively or to the people." And the supremacy of federal laws is limited to such as "shall be made in pursuance of the Constitution." The stares are co-equally supreme within their sphere; in no legal sense are they subordinate corporations.... To the states belong, not by virtue of the Federal Constitution but of their own sovereign power, the control of municipal and local government, the chartering of corporations, the statutory development and judicial administration of civil and criminal law, the supervision of religious bodies, the control of education insofar as it is not limited by the Fourteenth Amendment, and the general "police power" over the health, safety, and welfare of the people.[112]

Among the salient powers granted to the new government (in addition to powers granted previously over the post office, foreign affairs, etc.) were a limited taxing power, the judiciary, copyright laws, bankruptcy, and regulation of interstate and international commerce.

The constitution had to be ratified by each of the states. There the debate among federalists and antifederalists continued. The former argued that without the Constitution, there could be no Union and security was threatened by foreign territories to the North and South, and from beyond the Mississippi River.

The antifederalists argued that delegating to the central government both fiscal power and the power to regulate commerce would make it impossible for individuals to control the acts of government. In turn, the absence of control would lead to progressively increasing taxes.

For the antifederalists, this meant replacing the British tax collection that had led to independence with local taxation. They compared the voracity of the king with the voracity of their own government, and some warned about the risks of not limiting the power of governments. Robert Yeats, under the pseudonym of Brutus, wrote,

> But remember, when the people once part with power, they can seldom or never resume it again but by force. Many instances can be produced in which the people have voluntarily increased the powers of their rulers; but few, if any, in which rulers have willingly abridged their authority. This is a sufficient reason to induce you to be careful, in the first instance, how you deposit the powers of government.[113]

Robert Yeats also wrote that the most important limitation to government power is limitation of tax revenue. In fact, a government that does not have limits on tax collection will not have a limit on spending. This would produce deficits and would finance activities that violate individual rights.

> The legislature ... are the sole judges of what is necessary to provide for the common defense, and they only are to determine what is for the general welfare; this power therefore is neither more nor less, than a power to lay and collect taxes, imposts, and excises, at their pleasure; not only [is] the power to lay taxes unlimited, as to the amount they may require, but it is perfect and absolute to raise them in any mode they please.... In the business therefore of laying and collecting taxes, the idea of confederation is totally lost, and that of one entire republic is embraced. It is proper here to remark, that the authority to lay and collect taxes is the most important of any power that can be granted; it connects with it almost all other powers, or at least will in process of time draw all other after it; it is the great mean of protection, security, and defense, in a good government, and the great engine of oppression and tyranny in a bad one.[114]

This is one of many warnings issued by the antifederalist representatives. In truth, they were warning against a future risk that at some point, the prevailing tradition would be broken. George Clinton wrote,

> It is said that the opinions, uses and manners of the American people make them capable of resisting and preventing oppression, but it should be kept in mind that opinions, uses, and manners change, and they do not necessarily constitute obstacles against governmental trespasses.[115]

As a result of the actions of the antifederalists and the reluctance of the states to relinquish power to the Confederation, the Constitutional text included limitations on government and a practical vigilance of the actions of government. The fact that those charged with drafting the national constitution came from states that for a number of years had already had their own written equivalents acted as a limit to the national document.

As mentioned earlier, the need to attract and retain colonists was a consideration when the states passed their basic laws. Among the institutions protected were freedom of labor, of worship, and of the press; limited government; and low levels of taxation. When the national document was drafted, these traditions were not left out.

David S. Landes has attributed the explosion of productivity in

Europe between 1500 and 1800 to the development of markets and competition. Indeed, innovations such as the hydraulic wheel, the mechanic watch, gunpowder, and the printing press were known many centuries before their productivity was felt. To be sure, in competitive markets, it is necessary to adopt inventions that will increase productivity.

We can apply the model of private competition leading to technical improvements to the case of federalism in the United States at the end of the eighteenth century. Just as entrepreneurs responded to incentives to improve the technical instruments of their time, competition among states led to improvements in institutions.

Federalist Reforms, Centralist Habits

Before entering into a federal bond, the colonies in the United States had developed their own constitutions. Hispanic America, on the other hand, had been a single unit dominated by the King of Spain. This difference is key to understanding historical development of the new nations. In *The Centralist Tradition in Latin America*, Claudio Véliz identifies four factors on which the centralist nature of Latin American societies rests: the absence of the feudal experience; the absence of religious nonconformity and the ensuing centralism of a dominant religion; the absence of an event that over time could be the counterpart the European Industrial Revolution; and the absence of the ideological, political, and social developments associated with the French Revolution that drastically transformed Western Europe during the last 150 years.[116]

According to Véliz, federal arrangements and federalism itself were exotic transplants from distant political climates, more in line with heretic religions. Liberalism in South America had to be learned from books, some written in French, and others in English. In consequence, the constitutions drafted during this period were ephemerous and invariably designed by industrious intellectuals who were elevated to eminencies by their military heroes. But this was unrelated to everyday reality. The existence of the bureaucratic establishment meant that most of the controversies over the administrative arrangements of the republics were irrelevant. Throughout the periods of anarchy and violence what remained constant was the centralist structure of government in its different authoritarian incarnations. This was the only form of government known to the bureaucracy. The imaginative federal schemes, the audacious liberal constitutions, and the valiant attempts at decentralization during the early years of the republics shared something in common: they were all tried, but none succeeded.[117]

In Mexico, for instance, after General Santa Anna deposed Emperor Agustin I, a group of liberal intellectuals drafted a federal constitution that divided the territory of the former Viceroyalty of New Spain into 19 states and a number of minor regions. Stephen F. Austin presented Miguel Ramos Arizpe, in 1823, the synthesis of a federal constitution based entirely on that of the United States, and there is little doubt that it influenced the final text of the Mexican Federal Constitution. But in 1834, General Santa Anna came to power and enacted a conservative and centralist constitution. Lloyd Mecham wrote,

> Federalism has never existed in Mexico. It is commonly accepted today that the Mexican nation has been federal only in theory; it has actually always been centralist.[118]

TABLE 4-1
The Centralist Tradition in Latin America

	Latin America	United States
Origin of organization in America	Spanish imperial centralism	British customs. Self-government by the colonies
Delegation of power	Centralized states granted limited powers to the provinces	The states delegated specific functions to the federation
Direction of delegation	Top down	Bottom up
Competition among political units	No	Yes
Public debate, referendum and/or approval of the Constitution	Absent	Present
Fiscal power	Centralized	Federal
Tax collection	Centralized and later, redistributed	Local (*property tax*), state (*sales tax*) and federal (*income tax*)
Division of power	Formal, not effective	Formal and effective
Responsibility for the acts of government	Diffuse	Direct
Incentives for performance	Low	High

In the Provinces of the Río de la Plata, after a sequence of paternalistic republicanism and anarchic dissolution, Juan Manuel de Rosas came to power in 1830 with the strength of a federal program that had the support of the provinces. But in the name of federalism and the Catholic Church, and against "the savage Unitarians," he established the most centralized, nationalistic, and lasting regime the country ever saw.

In Brazil, Don Pedro I sanctioned a constitution that was in force until the establishment of the Republic in 1889. The Constitution of 1891 hardly represented a break with the country's centralist tradition.

Chile declared formal independence in 1818, and General Bernardo O'Higgins was appointed supreme director. In 1828, Chile adopted a federal constitution that supposedly included safeguards against the exercise of power. Yet the constitution did not transform a centralist country into a South American version of the United States. What it did was inspire the powerful, conservative, and centralist uprising that grabbed power.

The Argentine National Constitution of 1853 represented a fundamental break with the previous legal tradition. Its immediate impact was significant and the contradiction evident. The legal change, new ideas, the prevailing political situation (the defeat of Juan Manuel de Rosas), and the urgent need to conquer the desert all supported the new framework over the previous social order. Still the main concern of its author, Juan B. Alberdi, was that the previous laws not invalidate the new constitution.

> The constitution contemplated that what has existed for three centuries cannot be discarded by decree. A written law can be derogated in an instant, unlike an ingrained custom: in an instant, a single cannon discharge can destroy a monument that has existed for centuries, but all the gunpowder in the world would be impotent to destroy a general hereditary concern. The custom represents the law. The only way to derogate custom is through a law animated through time. At least a century of economic freedom will be necessary to destroy our three centuries of monopolistic and exclusive colonialism.[119]

Although the new countries adopted regimes ostensibly inspired by the Constitution of the United States, centralized government was not reformed, and checks and balances among the three branches were not in place. There was no proper division among the Executive, Legislative, and Judicial powers, with the latter being totally subservient to the Executive.

The Train of Progress

With the new Latin American nations better organized and more stable during the second half of the nineteenth century, the countries participated in the international economy. More advanced countries in the midst of the industrial revolution needed raw materials, which meant that Latin American economies could jump on the train to progress, attaining unusually high growth in their exports, production, and wages.

With Europe and the United States in the middle of industrialization, the period 1850 to 1914 was one of growth for the new nations. William Glade writes that during these years the global system reached its highest point. The gold standard, international trade, and international movements of capital and labor were freer than ever.[120]

In those years, European agriculture could not meet the demands of the urban populations for grains, wool, leather, and beef. There was strong pressure for resorting to more remote providers, and Europe looked further to less populated territories, such as Australia, New Zealand, Canada, South Africa, the mid-western and western regions of the United States, Argentina, Uruguay, and Southern Brazil. These areas were subsequently populated, and new production techniques were introduced to satisfy the European need for products.[121]

Critics of this period see it as a "new colonial pact," with Latin America producing raw materials destined for the centers of the new industrial economy and food products for the metropolitan areas. Perishable goods were no longer dominant in the exchanges. Investments assured a variable flow of capital goods, metal products, fuel, parts, and other complementary goods.[122]

Two factors marked the situation in Latin America: the higher availability of capital and the growing capacity of European cities to absorb Hispanic America's exports. The first one translated into investments and credits to governments. The political consequence of the availability of capital was to allow governments to increase revenues without relying on their usual (rural) sources of revenue. This contributed to the consolidation of the national states. In Argentina, where government revenues traditionally came from import duties from transatlantic trade, European loans meant that the central government could make decisions independently of the reluctant provinces. A finance minister had observed that toward the end of the 1870s the amount of the loans exactly covered the costs of civil wars and the war with Paraguay. Halperín Donghi states that loans to government were increasingly long term — placed by bankers in European stock exchanges, especially London — and rested on the assumption that constant expansion of the Latin American economies would take care of high levels of indebtedness.[123]

The expansion of the external sector was the primary source of government financing, as well as the guarantee for the foreign debt. A heavy tax regime on the domestic market was avoided by means of an implicit fiscal pact between the government and taxpayers based on indirect taxes, mainly levied on imports.

A small tax on imports did not seem a high price to pay for the public goods that an expanding society produced. This explains the fiscal pact between government and taxpayers and the wide consensus on fiscal burden that until 1930 allowed society to be governable.[124]

Another factor that facilitated the growth of the economies oriented toward European markets was the improvement in sea transportation. The introduction of the steam ship made access to foreign markets cheaper and faster. Between 1850 and 1910 tonnage of merchant fleets in the world quadrupled, and annual shipping capacity grew even more with the reduced time of travel. A voyage between Buenos Aires and Europe went from three to four months, to 50 to 60 days.[125]

Figures for international trade are even more impressive: in 1880 Argentine exports increased tenfold compared to the beginning of the century and multiplied by 50 the value of rural exports; Chile multiplied its exports by 50 during the same period. Growth in Brazil was more moderate (tenfold growth in exports at the beginning of the twentieth century); Venezuela exports increased sevenfold, Peru fivefold. Ecuador tripled its own while Bolivia's grew by only 75 percent and Mexico's by 20 percent.[126] Growth focused on the formerly marginal territories of the former Empire, which decreased the relevance of mining.[127]

The increases in exports were not the spontaneous response of the new economic organization of Latin American countries to opportunities in foreign markets. New factors—such as the railroads built to connect inland regions with seaports, new communications infrastructure installed to connect production areas with commercial centers of the country, new mining and agriculture production technologies, new public utilities, and port infrastructure—allowed the movement of people, goods, and information within reasonably modern structures.[128]

In 1913, almost one-third of all foreign investment in Latin America was invested in government debt. Railroad represented one-third of all direct investment (the remaining investments were spread among public utilities, mining, and to a smaller extent, agriculture, real estate, and manufacturing).[129] In the Argentine pampas, for the most part without navigable rivers, farm exploitation would become viable only after the railroad appeared on the scene. Railroads helped populate rural areas, brought production to ports, and in conjunction with lower shipping costs enabled the products to reach distant European markets. The cost of the railroads amounted to five full years of exports; so it fell on the government to finance construction with foreign debt. When the government ceded that role to private enterprise, it did so through licenses to foreign corporations.

Both the government and the investors assumed that the railroads would increase wealth, the debt would be repaid and profits made.[130]

TABLE 4–2
British Investments in Latin America in 1913

Country	Nominal Amount	Percent of Total
Argentina	1,860,700,000	37.34
Brazil	1,161,500,000	23.31
Mexico	807,622,000	16.21
Chile	331,691,000	6.65
Uruguay	239,727,000	4.81
Cuba	222,223,000	4.46
Peru	133,292,000	2.67
Guatemala	52,226,000	1.04
Venezuela	41,350,000	0.83
Colombia	34,470,000	0.69
Costa Rica	33,300,000	0.67
Honduras	15,716,000	0.32
Paraguay	15,579,000	0.31
Ecuador	14,505,000	0.29
El Salvador	11,124,000	0.22
Nicaragua	6,196,000	0.12
Bolivia	2,099,000	0.04
TOTAL	4,983,320,000	

Source: Max Winkler, Investments of United States Capital in Latin America, p. 280, quoted in William Glade, The Latin American Economies, p. 220.

During the period from 1850 to 1880 British investors played a direct role in the financing of 34 railroads and 24 public utilities companies, including municipal gas, light rail, and water providers. Also in this period, steam navigation companies and early telecommunication companies emerged, and declining amounts of capital were devoted to mining, banking, real estate, and meat processing. British investments doubled between 1900 and 1914. In 1914, Latin America was the recipient of approximately 20 percent of all British foreign investment.

Massive immigration to Argentina, Uruguay, and Central and Southern Brazil is another important feature of the second half of the nineteenth century. During the highest immigration period (1861–1920), approximately 45 million persons moved to the American continent. The majority went to the United States (61 percent); approximately 10 percent went to Argentina and 7 percent to Brazil. The rest of the Latin American countries received smaller percentages of immigrants.[131]

By 1870, the Argentine provinces had tripled their population from the beginning of the century to 1.8 million. Brazil had comparable growth and a population of 10 million. Chile had doubled its population in 1869 (to 2 million), Peru had 2.6 million inhabitants in 1876, Nueva Granada had 2.9 million in 1871 and Venezuela 1.8 million in 1873.

The image of stability that Latin American economies wanted to convey to investors is illustrated by mottoes such as "Peace and Administration," during the presidency of Julio A. Roca, and "Order and Progress" in the Brazilian flag. Free trade policies made possible new roles for Latin America in the world economy. Free trade is the common faith of political leaders and powerful domestic sectors, yet, in defense of specific interests, they can impose rules that are disconcerting to those who see both sides of purely intellectual doctrines.[132]

Some authors, among them Juan B. Alberdi, aware of the burden of colonial traditions and the relevance of informal institutions, stressed the importance of immigration as a means of renewing and discarding some of the perverse practices inherited from Spain. In the case of Argentina, non–Spanish immigration was high.

This period of economic certainty and growth in several Latin American economies was a win-win situation for the dominant local groups (income from natural resources), the government (fiscal revenues from growing international trade), and foreign investors (looking for markets for their products). Some factors capable of modifying entrenched colonial patterns of behavior entered these countries. For instance, foreign investment required predictability in the legal framework, which acted as a constraint on government. European immigration, especially from Italy, England, and Germany, brought new patterns of conduct. The need to export to highly competitive markets meant that domestic production and marketing techniques needed to improve in cooperation with the foreign investors.

Changes in international economic trade from the mid–1800s to the early decades of the 20th century modified the win-win game for businessmen and governments, both in Latin America and elsewhere. They also exposed weaknesses that had been overlooked during the expansion years, like the limited participation of the citizens in voting for elected officials.

Continuity or Institutional Change?

North comments that although the revolution gave birth to the United States, pre–Revolutionary history can only be understood in terms of the continuity of many formal and informal institutions, and of the enactment into laws of pre-existing limitations to political power.[133]

The Magna Carta of 1215, the Bill of Rights, the Glorious Revolution of 1688, the emigration of the Pilgrims, and the American Revolution can be construed as a seamless series of attempts at limiting the sovereign's power and expanding the sphere of individual decision-making.

Roberto Cortés Conde writes that the transition was easier for the United States, having inherited from Great Britain institutions of limited government with separation of powers. In Spain, and its colonies, the transitions of the nineteenth century were traumatic, from an absolutist to a constitutional regime. The Spanish American revolutions were marked by the difficult transition from the *ancien régime* to a modern one. Moreover, decisions had to be made as to whether the government would be centralized, or not, which in turn led to decades of ideological disagreement between centralists (*"unitarios"*) and federalists (*"federales"*) and a host of other problems, some left over from colonial times; some arose from regional conflicts, and some derived from geographical circumstances, such as transportation technology and the long distances.[134]

According to Glade the entrenched informal institutions that prevailed — Indian collectivism and Spanish interventionism — were repudiated and replaced with policies associated with economic liberalism. But the effort did not take into account the preexisting power structures and cultural conditions, which could not support the new ideology.[135]

In Latin America, the conquistadors imposed a uniform religion and an equally uniform bureaucratic administration on the existing agricultural society. Which group would exert control over the bureaucracy was an ongoing problem. Douglass North also notes that the importation of constitutions inspired by the United States did not have the intended effects. North refuted the notion that a society's institutional patterns can be modified through the enactment of positive statutes. Even when the rules are similar, enforcement mechanisms, rules of behavior, and the subjective models of acting agents are not. Therefore, the real incentive structures and the consequences of certain policies vary as well. For North, a common set of fundamental changes in relative prices or the imposition of a set of common rules will lead to quite different results in societies depending on their institutional rules.[136]

In the United States, the Constitution embodied the English heritage of political and economic rules, and later, the rules of the colonies, complemented by an ideological model consistent with the problems at hand. In Hispanic America, a new set of rules was superimposed on a centuries-old heritage of bureaucratic controls and its corresponding ideology. That is why both federalist schemes and decentralization efforts failed after independence.

Juan Bautista Alberdi was the contemporary Latin American thinker who wrote most clearly about the decisive role that informal institutions have in long-term economic performance. He considered the colonial legacy one of the major hurdles to long-term economic growth:

> The formerly Spanish America is poor from its very origin and, because of that origin that owes to a nation itself poor at the time of the discovery and conquest, due to a holy war that lasted eight centuries during which it forgot or learnt to ignore work, that is the sole source of wealth, just as its absence is the sole cause of poverty....
>
> America was conquered for the glory of its Crown and the broadening of its Catholic faith, freeing it from heathen and pagans, neither for industry or commerce, nor the welfare of its own people. If love for gold aided the conquest, it only determined the hordes of idle adventurers impoverished by the holy war against the Moors.
>
> The English emigrated to America in search of a factory, the Spaniards in search of a fortune.[137]
>
> It was not the workers that emigrated. It was not industry that reigned in the Peninsula, but the sword of the crusader, the altar of the priest, and the servant of the throne. Emigrants were military, noblemen, clergy, and employees of the Crown. Easy wealth, already formed, discovered, that can be obtained without the double effort of work and saving, is the wealth aspired to by the adventurer, the nobleman, the soldier, the sovereign.

One of Alberdi's main criticisms focuses on the rent-seeking posture of the Spanish crown and the artificiality of its apparent economic power, which was not based on wealth creation but on owning mineral resources and exploiting them with native slave labor.

> The Americans, that is, the natives, were not wealthy: gold and silver were in the depths of the earth, and it was only possible to extract them by working.... That work was carried out, not with European work but with American work, the work of the defeated native, not of the conquering European. The natives were later succeeded by black slaves introduced by white Europeans.
>
> Wealth so acquired was not the daughter of the virtues of work and savings, like the primitive Roman and Greek wealth; it was the daughter of coercion and injustice: a robbery of the soil by work robbed to man.[138]

According to Halperín Donghi, the situation in Latin America, at the same time united and extremely fragmented, is reminiscent of Europe in the sixteenth century, crisscrossed by a network of trade routes that overcame distances at a very high cost and inadequately communicated diminutive economic units. This transportation system continued to be the most viable alternative for the Hispanic America that was starting to emerge, divided into single production areas and economically tied to a transatlantic hub. The survival of the previous communications system itself shows to what extent this transformation of the colonies remained incomplete.

Finally, attempts at establishing a state within the liberal institutional frameworks proposed by the revolutionaries of 1810 ran against the cold reality of the administrative, legal, and cultural heritage of the colony. In spite of the constant reference to the United States Revolution of 1776, Latin America was neither republican nor federalist. The Executive power prevailed over the others, and the centuries-old tradition of centralism survived.

5
Rebirth and Decline of Interventionist Institutions (1930–1990)

In the 1930s, new ideas seduced politicians and legislators. The international situation led to the closing of international trade and the emergence of the welfare state. Constraints on private activity, reliance on public employment, and toeing the official line became enshrined in the law. Written rules that had triggered economic growth fell prey to the renewed strength of restrictive legislation.

Changes during the 1920s and 1930s weakened the close bond between the Latin American economies and some of the more advanced countries. The *Pax Britannica*—the economic order that prevailed during the nineteenth century—came to a close. Latin American countries had thrived as suppliers of raw materials for the Industrial Revolution, with some, like Argentina, surpassing European countries in per capita income. The relationship between the new Latin American nations and the old continent and, in some cases, the United States, had neutralized the colonial institutions inherited from Spain and Portugal. The primacy of free trade, the free movement of capital, and a monetary regime under the gold standard were accompanied by domestic peace, respect of private property rights, open international markets, and low levels of taxation and regulation.

But the foundation of the apparent institutional transformation that occurred in the nineteenth century was weak. It was not based on the evolution of usage, customs, and rules that protected individual liberty and restricted the power of government. It became clear as soon as international conditions changed that the transformation depended on constraints placed by international trade. It soon became obvious that (Spanish) informal institutions would prevail over formal ones (limited government).

Public choice theorist Charles Rawley writes that freedom is not a necessary element for wealth. Such is the case for the four Asian tigers—Taiwan, South Korea, Singapore, and Hong Kong—which exemplify the ability of autocracies to protect private property rights and increase the per capita income of its citizens. The economic freedoms on which their achievements rest will last only for the duration of the term of the benevolent dictator or the oligarchy that controls them.[139] In Latin America, repeated attempts to amend formal institutions through informal ones (uses, values and customs) achieved only temporary success.

The break had different manifestations. In the political arena, the 20th century was marked by instability in the rules of the game, populism, and the constant shift between civilian and military governments. In the economic arena, statism and regulation became the norm. Internationally, the prevailing view was one of a zero sum game in international relations between developed and undeveloped countries, the dominant idea being that poverty in Latin America was the counterpart of the wealth of developed countries. Legally, the pervasive social constitutionalism present in the region's legislation reflected the decline of individual and private property rights that had been established in the liberal constitutions and opened the door to the unlimited intervention of the state in the life of its citizens.

Latin America underwent a change in its relations with the rest of the world, in the thinking and in the policies implemented, and a sense of uncertainty prevailed regarding private property and the products it generated. The new rules of the game offered little incentive for entrepreneurial behavior; instead, rent-seeking activities were rewarded. It became more profitable to invest time and effort in influencing government officials to obtain privileges or protections than to go the difficult road of satisfying the consumer in an open market. Economies closed to imports, domestic production oriented to the local market, actual or potential conflicts with bordering nations—all of this meant that industries were shielded from foreign competition.

Decades of economic growth were followed by 30 years marked by one momentous economic crisis, two world wars, and a radical change in the formal rules of the developed countries that had bought our exports and originated foreign investment.

Although mainly a crisis for the United States, the crash of 1929 had important effects on Latin America. The United States had replaced England as the main source of foreign investment, and the recession had a huge impact on U.S. investment and trade with Argentina and the region. The widespread drop in GDP for the period 1928–1932 appears below.

TABLE 5-1
Decrease in GDP for Selected Countries, 1928–1932

Country	Percent
United States	28
Canada	29
Australia	9
Argentina	13
Brazil	7
Chile	30
Mexico	20
Venezuela	22
Peru	25

By the time World War II broke out, the constitutional continuity created through democratic elections had been lost. Unionization and the formation of powerful groups became more relevant for the formulation of economic policy, and most of the tools of the interventionist state were being implemented (from price controls, state-owned corporations, and currency exchange controls, to regulations on trade and import duties).

In the 1940s, countries all over the world faced the growing role of government in their economies. Government spending in Argentina as a percentage of GDP was 8 percent in 1870, similar to the average in developed countries (8.8 percent), but much higher than in the United States (3.9 percent). By 1937 the figure was up to 18 percent and would continue to grow steadily to 30 percent.[140]

World War II and the resulting decrease in international trade coincided with the spread of economic nationalism throughout Latin America. Foreign corporations were nationalized, and government agencies started making decisions previously made by the market. The reduction in imports of essential raw materials (like petroleum, coal, and iron ore) increased pressure from intellectuals and businessmen for domestic industrialization. Shortages could be mitigated if the industrial sector were developed, even if it had to be accomplished through government protection.

Autarky and protectionism in Europe, exacerbated by the war, damaged Latin American exports of agricultural food products. Toward the end of the 1950s, with the establishment of the European Community, self-sufficiency policies, implemented as direct or indirect subsidies (through barriers to trade), became more prevalent to the point of representing over two-thirds of the Community budget for four decades. The European officials' decision to subsidize their own agricultural sectors meant that the biggest consumer of Latin American farm products was out of the market.

In a period of only 20 years, external events, prevailing ideas, and a growing corporativism in society forced the creation of the instruments of interventionism: public agencies; price, wages and exchange controls; regulations; subsidies; public spending; and statutory protection of actual or alleged less favored sectors of society. In a short time these instruments would become the formal institutions that would modulate and recycle the old habits of the government and the population.

The new institutional structure became so internalized by the population that for decades there were no public policies that did not include one or more of these instruments. It was unthinkable to solve an economic policy problem without subsidies, control, bans, or direct public spending. The development of these institutions was uncoordinated, more reactive than the result of a calculated plan.

In the years that followed the crisis of 1930, the individual, formerly the minimal unit of Latin American political systems, was replaced by the nation, a new unit colonized by rent- and privilege-seeking interest groups who preached ideological nationalism. In the decades that followed, the state and not the market led the economy.

Interventionist Legislation

The constitutions enacted during the nineteenth century in the nascent Latin American countries were a combination of the ideals of the North American Revolution and the codifying mechanisms of the French Revolution. The presidential regimes were the natural successors to the regional *caudillos*, which, in contrast to the United States, did not have a Supreme Court to limit its absolute power.

Still, in spite of the strong centralist tradition, the republican constitutions were in force from the second half of the nineteenth to the early decades of the twentieth century. Changes in the international situation and the ensuing changes in economic policy, as well as the broadening of the electoral base, made it imperative to legislate those measures that conflicted with the classical liberal constitutions and their goal of protecting citizens against the absolute power of government.

Social constitutionalism replaced liberal constitutionalism in the midst of explosive social demands from the recently opened electoral systems. A. F. Cesarino Junio, representing this new school, wrote in *La organización social y económica en la Constitución brasileña del 18 de septiembre de 1946* that while "liberal democracy" protects the rights of the individual against the power of the state, a "social democracy" obliges the state and society to ensure a decent standard of living for citizens. This "new" constitutionalism enabled the open transfer of resources "from the rich to the poor," legalizing a mechanism that previously would have been considered a violation of rights.

Charles Rawley writes about the misconception that exists in Third World countries regarding the function of constitutions. When they do have constitutions they tend to be poorly organized and their enforcement is even worse. They fail to protect individual and civil liberties and show an absolute ignorance of the concept of economic freedom. He adds that Third World countries are impoverished and lack freedom, not because of bad luck or having insufficient resources, but because of the deliberate design of dictators, oligarchies, and single party systems that control their destinies. For the majority, redemption lies exclusively in the hands of these leaders or in those of the citizens who carry out successful revolutions.[141]

Social rights arise from labor relations and from the existence of intermediate structures of society such as family, schools, and unions, with particular emphasis on reducing inequalities and protecting the poor.[142] The Mexican Constitution of 1917 was the first one to add an extensive chapter on social rights. It was followed by most Latin American countries: Peru in 1923 and 1979; Argentina in 1949; Brazil in 1934, 1937, 1946, and 1969; Cuba in 1960; Venezuela in 1961; and Ecuador in 1979. (Some European countries made similar changes: Portugal in 1976, Spain in 1978, and Italy in 1946.)

The amended constitutions included rules on minimum wage, maximum work hours, paid vacations, the right to strike, rules regarding women at work, the right to unionize, etc. In the new framework, private property rights are not absolute, but are dependent on the common good or general welfare, as the case may be. The "social role" of constitutions placed limits on individual rights and legalized takings of property for a public purpose.

Social constitutionalism also involved the inclusion in formal constitutions of a bill of social and economic rights, and rules on education, culture, family, work, professional or union associations, property rights, the economy, childhood issues, the elderly, social security. It also addressed *social issues*, such as the relation of individuals and work, the relation between capital and labor, social classes and the factors of production, employers and workers, unions and the state.

These constitutional changes were vital in encouraging populist regimes. Work, for example, stopped being an individual right and became a duty of the state, "a calling inherent to human nature — to work is to live and without work, life on Earth would be impossible."[143] The constitutional formalization of social rights triggered the social struggle for a larger piece of the pie, which itself became smaller and smaller.

Maurice Duverger explored how the new social constitutionalism gave rise to new agencies and powers of the state that delineated the new corporative state. For example, the Peruvian Constitution of 1933 is the first in Spanish America to create a National Economic Council, "made up of representatives of consumers, capital, labor and the liberal professions." The Brazilian Constitution of 1937 was the instrument that gave Getulio Vargas the legal power to build O Estado Novo (the New State) and provided for the establishment of an Economic Council that would represent the country's production sectors. A new role for the state in guiding the economy was recognized in the constitutions of Guatemala (1956), Venezuela (1961), Uruguay (1966), and Panama (1972). In 1978, the Constitution of Ecuador established a National Council on Development (sections 89, 90, and 91) "in order to set forth general economic and social policy and implement the corresponding development plans."[144]

The truth ultimately came out through the informal economy. The absence of mandatory compliance with the legal norms allowed the development of an underground economy, especially in the labor market. Unionization and rigid labor laws suffocated the market, and gradually, the black market became an essential component of Latin American life.[145]

The system of market prices continued to prevail in voluntary individual transactions, which were banned by statute. Poverty in Latin America grew under a legal system that was well-intentioned but ignored the natural laws that govern exchanges among individuals.

Social constitutionalism eliminated the last formal hurdle standing in the way of the return of the Leviathan. Four and a half centuries after the unification of the kingdoms of Castile and Aragon, Latin America showed little progress in taming absolute power.

Poverty in Latin America and Wealth in Central Countries

The drop in international demand during the 1930s focused attention on the lower prices for *commodities* exported by Latin America and its counterpart, the higher prices of industrial products exported by more advanced economies. The drop in prices affected sugar production from

5. Rebirth and Decline of Interventionist Institutions (1930–1990)

Cuba to Peru, agriculture and livestock in the Río de la Plata, Chilean saltpeter, and Brazilian coffee, among others.

This phenomenon was described from a broader theory of the relation between central and peripheral countries. Just as the publication in 1932 of John Maynard Keynes' *General Theory of Employment, Interest, and Money* was the theoretical foundation of many economic policies implemented during the Depression, the writings of Raúl Prebisch for the Economic Commission for Latin America (ECLAC) were the theoretical model used by the region's governments. Both civilian and military governments shared the ideal of industrial development for their countries as a way to escape the unfair relationship between the center and the periphery.

The ECLAC studied the relations between Latin America and industrial economies during the 1930s and 1940s and in its *Estudio económico de Latin America, 1949*, made three main points:[146] 1) Latin America's ability to import from central economies had suffered steadily after World War I because of the diminution in its exports and, more so, because of the unfavorable terms of exchange; 2) imports by central economies depend more on their development than on trade with peripheral economies; 3) "if on account of a lower national income or restrictions on imports by the United States and Great Britain, the lower prices do not seem to increase imports; rather, it allows central economies to destine a lower proportion of their monetary income to the acquisition of those imports."[147]

While the foreign demand for raw materials had an income elasticity lower than one (which determined that exports from periphery to the center would increase at a lower rate than income growth in the latter), demand for manufactured products had an income elasticity higher than one (which determined that exports of manufactured products to the periphery grew at a rate higher than the income of the latter). Thus, the growth rate of the products of the periphery was condemned to being lower than the growth rate in the central economy.

The deterioration of the terms of exchange was perceived to be an expression of the structural features of the periphery. Since the production of raw materials—Latin America's exports—grew faster than demand, prices fell continually. On the other hand, the region imported manufactured products, demand for which grew faster than income and exports, giving rise to continuous trade deficits.

The prescriptions of the ECLAC openly questioned the "international division of labor" enunciated by Adam Smith in *The Wealth of Nations*. Prebisch set out to refute the theory, and his statement became known as the "the Prebisch thesis." He starts from a disparity in economic growth in more advanced nations (the center in his terminology) compared to that in developing countries (the periphery). The former support themselves through technological progress, while the latter supply raw materials for the industrial centers. The problem is that communities in the periphery have not profited from the benefits of technological progress as much as the countries in the center. He goes on to add that improvements in productivity achieved in the peripheral economies have benefited the center. Prebisch wrote that the validity of Smith's formulation presupposes that participating economies are strictly complementary, but countries that participate in international trade have specific differences in structure and functions. Therefore, trade between countries in the periphery and the center — based on exports of raw materials and manufactured goods, respectively — will preclude economic development of the former.[148] The way out of the "periphery of raw materials" was "industrialization."

A more emotional (and more influential in Latin America) formulation of international trade as a zero-sum game came from Eduardo Galeano, in *Las venas abiertas de America Latina*:

> There are two sides to the international division of labor: one group of countries specialized in winning, and the other, in losing. Our piece of the world, which we call Latin America, specialized in losing early on, from the times when the Europeans of the Renaissance took to the sea and buried their teeth in our throat.... We are still servicing the needs of others, with our reserves of oil and iron, copper, beef, fruits and coffee, destined to the rich countries that gain through their consumption more than Latin America gains producing them.[149]

This vision permeated the original analysis by the ECLAC, focused almost exclusively on commercial transactions, that is, the specialization (raw materials and manufactures) imposed or resulting from the unequal spreading of economic and technological progress. The original analysis did not mention any of the features and implications of the financial links established by foreign credit and investment.[150]

The "center-periphery" theory gave rise to the theory of dependence, expressed mainly in sociological terms. Fernando H. Cardoso, who would later become president of Brazil, in his 1970 paper, "Development and dependence: theoretical perspectives in sociological analysis," proposed replacing the terminology of "central" and "peripheral" economies with "developed" and "underdeveloped." Underdevelopment describes a state or degree of differentiation of the productive system, without stressing control on production and consumption decisions, either internally (socialism, capitalism, etc.) or externally (colonialism, periphery of world markets, etc.). The notions of center and periphery underline the role of underdeveloped economies in the world market, without any reference to the political and social aspects of dependence. The notion of dependence alludes directly to the existence and functioning of the economic and political systems, as well as the relations between the two, both domestically and externally.[151]

The main economic policy recommendation emerging from that diagnosis was industrialization — seen as the only viable means for peripheral or marginal countries to attain adequate income levels. The ECLAC formulated a *dirigiste* model to foster industrialization, provide for employment, increase productivity, and overcome external deficits. Just as many other populist proposals in those days, the model was nationalistic, popular, and statist, and proposed social and economic changes that aimed at gradually boosting the economic and social participation of marginal and poor classes.[152]

Even the failed attempt to establish a Latin American free trade zone originated with the ECLAC, as an alternative to foreign dependence. Juan Vacchino, in *Integración Latinoamericana. De la ALALC a la ALADI*, explained the model's proposals that balanced foreign trade and stopping the decline of the terms of exchange could be achieved through substantial transformations in the structure of foreign trade: expanding exports of raw materials at a pace that reflected the need for foreign currency, diversification of exports — which would gradually include manufactured products — and a modification in the composition of imports.

Regional integration ranked high among the instruments and mechanisms of industrialization, together with the creation of a public sector and the implementation of a rational and efficient economic policy that would guide and protect national industries. It was meant to be a tool of economic independence and development that would help overcome international oppression and deepen the process of industrialization.

In the negotiations that preceded the Treaty of Montevideo in 1960, the GATT Secretary did not look favorably on the project developed by the ECLAC's working group, explaining that their model risked establishing custom or trade preferences — a type of discrimination that was not allowed among countries that were members of GATT — without the assurance that it would create a free trade zone in a reasonable period of time.[153]

Eduardo Galeano described this view of the zero-sum game:

> For those who view History as a struggle, the backwardness and poverty of Latin America are the result of its failure: we lost, they won. But the

> winners won because we lost. The history of Latin America's underdevelopment, I repeat, is the history of the development of world capitalism. Our defeat has always been implicit in their victory; our wealth generated our poverty and fed the prosperity of others: the empires and their native agents. In the neocolonial alchemy, gold becomes base metal, and food, poison.
>
> Potosí, Zacatecas and Ouro Preto fell from the heights of the splendors of precious metals to the depths of depleted mines. Ruin was the destiny of the Chilean saltpeter pampas, the rubber of the Amazon forest, the sugar plantations of Northeastern Brazil, the Argentine *quebrachos*. Some oil villages in Maracaibo have painful reason to believe in the mortality of fortunes that nature grants and imperialism usurps. The rain that irrigates the centers of imperial power drowns the vast suburbs of the system. In a parallel way, the welfare of our dominant classes— dominant internally, dominated from outside — is the curse of our multitudes, condemned to lives as beasts of burden....
>
> New factories are built in the privileged poles of development — São Paulo, Buenos Aires, Mexico City — reducing more and more the amount of labor needed. The system did not anticipate this small problem: there are more people than jobs. People reproduce. They make love enthusiastically and without precautions. Increasingly, people are stranded along the sides of the road, jobless in the countryside, with its gigantic, idle land estates; jobless in the city, where machines reign; the system vomits men.[154]

Universities and academic centers developed "Latin American" theories that supported varied government actions. If the stated objective was "industrial development," the "national state" was to be its implementing arm.

Political Instability: Populism and Militarism

Lack of consensus on the basic societal rules was manifested in the political arena through the emergence of populist regimes, military regimes, and populist-military regimes. Constant changes in administrations meant changes in economic policies and legal uncertainty. The "civilian-military pendulum," as this period has been called by some authors, oscillated widely from regimes that bordered on nazi-fascism, such as the Perón regime, and others self-described as socialist, like Fidel Castro's.

Agrarian reforms, takings of property, and nationalization of corporations were common. The lack of consistency and continuity of these policies is best exemplified by Argentina's 1960s oil policy, which first awarded concessions for oil exploration and exploitation and subsequently proceeded to cancel them, all in the short period of five years.

In the economic sector, every change in the rules of the game introduces an element of uncertainty about future prices, adding to the risk, and a greater profitability requirement for investments. This is why the most successful investments of the period are related to government purchases and protected sectors of the economy, where the regulatory protections afforded a level of profitability that covered the higher risk.

A clear indicator of political instability is the number of presidents that Latin American countries had between 1950 and 1990. Argentina had 19 presidents, roughly one every two years. Brazil had 23 presidents and Bolivia 16. Among the more "stable" countries, Chile had 7 presidents (one of which, Augusto Pinochet, ruled for 17 years), Peru 9, Uruguay 14, and Mexico 8.

The regimes of Vargas and Perón provide clear examples of populist policies—an open redistribution of income from the agricultural and export sectors generated the unlimited support of the masses. In Mexico, the official party PRI, created in 1929, adopted the characteristics of revolutionary parties, advocating the destruction of the dominant class and the formation of a new productive system, with new privileges for economic groups and welfare policies for the masses.

The number of military *coups d'état* grew starting in the mid–1950s, and military intervention in politics became a phenomenon in itself, giving rise to such notions as military interventionism, authoritarianism, and militarism itself. Norberto Bobbio and Nicola Matteucci explained that in the Latin American sense, militarism evokes an excess. It refers to the excessive intervention of the armed forces in politics, which was frequent and prejudicial to prevailing legality.[155] The authors distinguish among various types of Latin American militarism from the more dictatorial—Somoza, Stroessner, Castelo Branco—to those more moderate in nature and aimed at rebuilding the system—such as Alfred Stepan in Brazil—where the military intervened to correct populist "excesses" that are perceived to be out of control."

Militarism and the participation of the armed forces in extramilitary affairs of society are a deeply ingrained tradition in Latin American history. In *Militares y sociedad en America Latina*, John J. Johnson wrote that the military in Hispanic America found in the models of industrialization and development an excellent theoretical justification for action, allowing them to draw a direct link between industrialization and state intervention. State intervention in the economy was the result of attempts to accelerate economic expansion. This rested on three premises: 1) industry could not survive without protection against foreign competition and only the state can provide that protection; 2) since private capital accumulation is slow, the state (which can accumulate capital more quickly through taxation and foreign borrowing) must intervene in the industrial sphere to attain the highest possible development levels; and 3) concern about the workers requires that the state control prices for basic necessities.[156] Military officials' interest in economic and public welfare schemes also arose from their desire to have access to a kind of economic power that they would not have attained by themselves.

For Johnson, nationalism in its broadest sense takes so many forms in Latin American societies that it would be impossible to ascertain whether civilians or the military are more nationalistic. Some generalizations can be made: cultural nationalism is practically a civilian monopoly. Economic nationalism is a notion supported by civilians and by the military; the latter usually respond emotionally rather than rationally when the control of natural resources is at stake, or are in danger of depletion, or when foreigners invest in "strategic" sectors of the economy. Legal nationalism — a concern for direct or indirect threat to national sovereignty — is ultimately a concern of the armed forces.[157]

From the 1930s to the 1990s, an important element of civilian-military relations has been the latent tension between the need for civilian governments to maintain armed forces for regulating foreign policy and keeping domestic order, on the one hand, and preventing those forces from usurping political power, on the other.

Political scientist Alfred Stepan studied the relationship between weak institutional stability in Latin America and military intervention in politics. He had written that the very absence of strong political institutions in most Latin American countries made different sectors of society strive to secure the support of the military as additional justification for the pursuit of their political objectives. Society is praetorian, in the sense that all its institutions (the Church, worker, and student groups) are highly politicized. So are the military and all the other groups that attempt to gain their support to augment their own political power.[158]

The military had been asked to intervene in Latin American life to moderate political activity and at the same time were denied the right to guide the direction of change within the political system. In most Latin American countries, the military had the power to play a moderating role in the political system in times of crisis. "Moderating power" has a specific meaning in this region. In colonial times, the viceroy had the constitutional right to intervene during political crises to avoid damage to institutions. Many scholars warned that the moderating power traditionally held by the viceroy was passed onto the military, legitimizing to a certain degree the exercise of that role by the military. Even many groups that were culturally anti-military accepted the legitimacy of that role.

Starting in the 1960s, a new militarism arose that has been called "techno-militarism." Duverger wrote that the new military or techno-military regimes (Brazil in 1964, Argentina 1966 and 1976, Chile 1973, and Uruguay 1973) have had different attitudes toward the constitutional issue. Initially, the *juntas* of commanders in chief declare their allegiance to the constitution. Later, by "institutional charters" (Brazil), the "charter of the revolution" (Argentina), and the "constitutional charter of the Junta" (Chile), the rights of citizens are altered, restricted or suspended, and certain political bodies are suspended as well, subordinating the constitutional text to the rules issued by the ruling military authorities.[159]

To this day, the armed forces are deeply ingrained Latin American institutions. Even though the region has been democratized, the military still has a relevant (formal or informal) role in domestic policy.

The End of the Party and the Decline of Interventionist Institutions

The expansion of the functions and powers of government also meant an increase in public spending. Government resorted to all the usual sources of public financing and then depleted other sporadic sources as well.

Section four of the Argentine National Constitution of 1853 briefly outlined a structure for financing the public sector: "The federal government shall provide for the expenses of the Nation with the funds of the National Treasury, made up of revenues from import and export duties, the sale or lease of federal lands, income from the Postal Services, and other contributions that Congress may levy on the population in an equitable and proportional manner." This list enumerated financing sources to which could be added the issue of debt certificates.

Traditional financing sources for the public sector are taxes, domestic and foreign debt, and monetary emission. Latin American countries resorted to all of these sources in increasing amounts in order to finance both the ever-growing public spending as well as transfers to the private sector. Taxes as a share of total revenues increased, until they reached their limit in the 1980s. Eventually, increases in tax rates failed to bring proportional increases in revenue due to tax evasion and disincentives to economic activity.

Furthermore, the growing need for revenues led the different administrations to create inconsistent tax sources. The resulting complexity reduced productivity of the economy, which in turn made for lower revenue collections.

Argentina resorted to all of the taxable bases. Initially, the bulk of tax receipts came from foreign trade, through tariffs on imports and exports. Later, specific consumption taxes were levied on alcohol, tobacco, luxury products, fuels, etc. In the 1930s, a temporary tax on gains was established—which would later become the income tax currently in force. Corporate assets, personal assets, salaries and wages, paid interest, value added, sales, consumption of public utilities, contracts, inheritances, more specific consumption, such as tickets to entertainment shows, did not escape the collecting arm of the Finance Secretaries. Still, the state kept growing, and this meant looking to other financing sources.

Historically, resorting to public debt had been frequent, especially to foreign debt, due to the size of international capital markets. In the 1970s, international liquidity—resulting from oil income from the OPEC countries (due to the oil crisis)—meant that the region's economies could be financed with lower interest rates. But financial circumstances changed in the following decade, and in conjunction with the lower-than-expected productivity of the projects that originated the loan gave rise to the so-called debt crises in Latin America. When oil prices fell, Mexico stopped paying its foreign debt service, devalued its currency, converted savings in dollars to Mexican pesos (cheating savers of the value of their savings), and, ultimately, nationalized the banking system.[160] First Mexico, and later Peru, Venezuela, Brazil, and Argentina stopped making capital and later interest payments on their foreign debts. Some countries even demanded "political treatment" of the debt aimed at obtaining both substantial pardons of the debts and also extending repay periods. Juan Carlos Casas writes that the long-term foreign debt grew six and a half times from 1970, when Latin American countries lamented their limited access to financial markets, to 1982, when one by one they started to default on their payments.[161]

With these developments, the voluntary loan market (banks, investors and funds) disappeared for these countries. Only small credit lines were available through multinational credit agencies such as the IMF, the IDB, and the World Bank.

TABLE 5-2
Latin American Debt Growth (in $US Millions)

Year	1970	1982
Total debt	56,323	333,310
Long term	27,995	238,349
National	15,992	178,078
Private (unsecured)	11,873	62,771
FMI	128	2,940
Short term	463	91,922

Source: Juan Carlos Casas, op. cit., from David Knox, "Latin American Debt-Facing Facts," Oxford International Institute, 1990.

The excessive reliance on foreign borrowing, especially under the favorable conditions prevailing in the 1970s, meant that the countries over-borrowed. Repaying the loans became technically impossible when conditions changed the following decade. In the early 1980s, the United States sharply increased its military public spending during the arms race with the USSR. That increase was financed primarily in the capital markets, putting considerable upward pressure on the interest rates. Credit became scarce and more expensive, and the international rate crept up to 20 percent annually, compared to 4 percent during the 1970s. Some highly indebted countries were unable to repay their foreign loans. Mexico, followed by Peru, Argentina, and Brazil, declared unilateral moratoriums, which endangered their ability to borrow in the future.

The prominent role of state-owned corporations, the regulatory maze, and the absence of price systems—all but destroyed by inflation—meant that the foreign debt funds were unprofitable. In many cases, the loans were applied to current expenses with low or no productivity. Eventually, the unprofitable investments reduced the ability to repay the debt. For some countries, Mexico being an example, the combination of less favorable international conditions and the inefficient allocation of the moneys borrowed led to an almost terminal crisis.

Fiscal insolvency was also reflected in the use of monetary emission as a source of financing. In Argentina the "inflationary tax" represented 61 of every 100 pesos collected by the state during the period 1982–85, reaching almost 18 percent of GDP. In 1989, 46 of every 100 pesos collected corresponded to the inflationary tax, and the rest, to statutory taxes.[162]

The growing tendency to print currency without a corresponding demand for it generated strong inflationary pressures that destroyed the monetary symbols of the region and generated meaningless price systems and inefficient allocation of resources. In Bolivia (1985), Argentina (1989),

Brazil and Peru (1991), rampant hyperinflation led to the abrupt start of the reform processes.

Toward the end of the decade, the die had been cast. The decrease in demand for currency by the public was the final blow to attempts at inflationary financing. The higher the issuing of currency (usually to finance public spending), the more the public responded by resorting to buying goods or foreign currency (dollars), which in turn led to exponential price increases.

In this environment, political uncertainty, social problems, and disputes over power added fuel to the fire. And the fire was well underway: the state was bankrupt, financial sources were drained, and inflation as a way out was not viable.

In February of 1990, in the midst of Argentina's inflation, Enrique Szewach wrote, "A necessary condition for hyperinflation is a credibility crisis in the State and its most representative symbol, the currency. The flight from domestic currency evidently has strong economic elements, in essence, an actual or potential fiscal imbalance that cannot be financed through public debt, but its root is eminently political in nature, if we define as political the loss of the government's authority/power."[163]

Economic indicators for Latin America during the 1980s speak for themselves: stagnation and hyperinflation; reductions in per capita GDP; declines in health, education, and justice; destruction of pension systems; complete absence of public investment (and its consequences on the quality of services); corruption; and ruin of state-owned corporations. It is no wonder that the 1980s are known throughout Latin America as "the lost decade."

6
The Rent-Seeking of the 1990s

We now turn to the question of whether the economic reforms that Latin American countries undertook during the 1990s—earlier in the case of Chile—constituted a shift away from the formal and informal institutions that were responsible for the poor economic performance of the region throughout most of its history.

Is it possible, in a single decade, to change legal traditions, customs, and values that for centuries guided political, social, and economic exchanges? The optimist sees in the reforms of the 1990s a capitalist revolution in Latin America; the pessimist is more cautious in evaluating the depth of the reforms.

But first, what were the reasons behind the reforms? Hyperinflationary crises and foreign debt crises that pointed toward the failure of the prevailing economic model triggered some of the reforms. The inflationary and fiscal crisis brought about by Salvador Allende in Chile in 1973, the Mexican foreign debt crisis of 1982, hyperinflation in Bolivia in 1985 and in Argentina in 1989—these events are landmarks in the history of the Latin American reforms and are the starting point of a search for solutions. These are the events that eventually would lead to privatizations, attempts at fiscal balance, deregulation of domestic markets, and an opening to international trade and investment. These goals were pursued and achieved at different rates, with Chile being at the most reformed end and Uruguay and Venezuela the ones to change the least. It is not chance that the countries that suffered the gravest crises attained the most dramatic reform in their economic institutions. The most salient features of the economic reform policies were their fiscalist orientation and the preeminence of institutional frameworks that aimed at seeking rents from economic activity, especially in privatization.

We can draw a parallel between the modern Latin American crises and Spain in the sixteenth century when the appropriation of the mineral wealth of the New World postponed the fiscal crisis of the monarchy, which otherwise — as was the case in England in the seventeenth century — would have forced the Crown to grant greater freedoms to its subjects. As a consequence, the goal of political organization in Spanish America was the administration and exploitation of the rents of the Crown and its "associates." The lack of limits on the monopoly use of force made the state an instrument for seeking fiscal revenue and rents, that is, non-competitive profits.

Roberto Cortes Conde alluded to the fiscalist orientation of the economic reforms when writing about the privatization of public utilities in Argentina. After decades of terrible service, most utilities were privatized during the 1990s. The privatized corporations found consumers with unmet demand and willing to pay higher prices for services. Both the corporations and the national state captured rents from the privatizations. The state — by allowing higher fees to be charged to consumers — was able to exact a higher price for the licensing of the services and the sale of the assets.[164] Cortés Conde adds that for decades, Argentines became adept at devising methods for obtaining economic rents from the state. This investment in time and resources, in getting to know procedures and the right persons, led to the creation of powerful interest networks.[165]

Douglass North explains very clearly the incentives in Third World countries, generated by the persistence of institutional frameworks that favor wealth distribution activities over wealth-creating ones. The incentives work to sustain monopolies and restrict competition, reducing opportunities for productive activity. Transaction costs can be so high as to constrain trade altogether. Only informal or black market activities and those operating with government protection and support will persist.[166]

During the 1980s, five Latin American economies — Peru, Bolivia, Argentina, Uruguay, and Brazil — returned to elected democracies after periods of military governments. Later, General Stroessner was deposed in Paraguay, and Augusto Pinochet was replaced in Chile by Patricio Aylwin's administration. In Central America, the Sandinista dictatorship lost the elections. In Mexico, the ruling PRI had to resort to fraud to ensure yet another administration. Throughout the continent pressure mounted for return to democracy.[167] But beyond the political sphere, and with the exceptions of Bolivia and Chile, there was little economic improvement.

For most of the 1980s and the early 1990s, the policies adopted were relatively more open than the prevailing accepted opinion. State intervention, autarky, and the lack of macroeconomic balance slowly gave way to a new framework that, although not fully open and competitive, represented progress in terms of respect for markets.

TABLE 6-1
Index of Economic Freedom[168]

		1995	2000
1	Chile	2.60	2.04
2	Argentina	2.85	2.23
3	Paraguay	2.94	3.01
4	Uruguay	3.03	2.50
5	Mexico	3.10	3.09
6	Bolivia	3.21	2.61
7	Ecuador	3.39	3.14
8	Peru	3.59	2.64
9	Brazil	3.46	3.46

In the above table (6-1), except for Chile the countries which suffered greatest economic turmoil in the eighties were Argentina, Bolivia and Peru, which introduced economic reforms early in the decade.

This transformation in economic orientation was the result of a combination of factors, among them the failure of the prevailing economic models in Argentina, Brazil, and Peru in the mid-'80s and the realization that the strategy of development based on the state had lost support. Many observers and political leaders realized that unorthodox plans were the last chance for state-based development programs to show some results in a new economic era. When these policies failed, politicians turned to the sources for help. The formidable performance of the East Asian economies provided an example worth studying and even imitating. Multilateral agencies provided consulting services and other programs. Also, a large group of professional economists contributed to a convergence of doctrinal positions.

Other examples were the considerable success of the Chilean reforms and the experience of Felipe González in Spain, which included competition, markets, and modernization. Finally, the dissolution of the USSR had enormous influence on those who had defended the substitution of market mechanisms with *dirigisme* and central planning.

Sebastian Edwards writes that the pillars on which consensus was founded were the need to stabilize the macroeconomy, open the economy, and reduce the role of the state in the production process.

Reasons for the Latin American Reforms

The Latin American reform processes share a common denominator, in that they were preceded by similar starting conditions for a relatively similar period of time. (Chile is the exception, with economic reforms dating back to 1975 because of a political crisis of a different nature.) For the rest of the countries in the region, acute inflationary processes (hyperinflationary in some cases) were the catalysts for the reforms, or serious problems with balance of payments due to the large foreign debts incurred.

In Argentina, for instance, the hyperinflationary crisis did not even allow for the development of a policymaking team and was responsible for costly losses in time and political friction. The seriousness of the situation also meant that the reform processes were not "attenuated" and did not contemplate their impact on those with lower incomes. There was some resistance among those groups that would be losers under the new conditions, and among those who would have a harder time adjusting to the new situation.

In those countries in which the reforms started in the midst of hyperinflation, the main task at hand was to re-establish confidence in the local currency. Any indicator that even hints at depreciation reduces the demand for currency and can easily produce the inflationary impulse. Demand for currency by the public became a powerful constraint for monetary policy makers. Fear and the possibility of a return to inflation made the reforms last and generated support that was confirmed in the voting booth in Argentina, Brazil, and Peru.

Economic reform processes differed from the structural reforms already under way. Economic reforms are monetary and fiscal measures to restore order to public finances. In the short term, they are adopted to secure access to financing and guarantees, mainly from international credit agencies. These measures usually include nominal salary freezes, adjustment of the exchange rate, reduction of public spending (particularly in personnel and current expenses), adjusting the prices of public goods and services to reflect market prices, an increase in the real interest rate, and an increase in taxation and genuine public revenues.

Structural reforms, on the other hand, aim to modify institutional patterns and basic rules of economic behavior. They attempt to redefine the role of the state in the economy (by privatizing and selling off state assets) and achieve a greater integration of the domestic economy in world markets; they pursue generalized deregulation of all markets to foster a culture of competition, and, in general, try to move the rent-seeking economy in a more productive direction.[168]

TABLE 6-2
Chronology of Reforms and Catalysts for Reforms, by Country

Country	Reforms Started	Reason for Reform/Catalyst	Inflation * (in %)	Dx/GDP* (in %)
Early reformers				
Chile	1975	Political crisis, foreign debt		66
Bolivia	1985	Hyperinflation	8170	
Mexico	1985/86	Debt crisis, inflation	105.7	62
Second wave of reformers				
Costa Rica	1988	Debt crisis	104	
Jamaica	1987/88	Debt crisis	8.9	157
Trinidad y Tobago	1987/88		8.3	38
Uruguay	1987/88	Inflation, Foreign debt	58	58
Third wave of reformers				
Argentina	1990/91	Hyperinflation	5900	30
Brazil	1991	High inflation	1584	31
Colombia	1990/91		32.4	35
El Salvador	1989/90		19.3	33
Guatemala	1992		10.2	26
Guyana	1989	Debt crisis	—	500
Honduras	1990	Debt crisis	36.4	109
Nicaragua	1990	Hyperinflation, debt, political crisis	13,490	600
Panama	1992	Foreign debt	1.2	114
Paraguay	1991–92	Regional agreement	11.8	27
Peru	1991	Hyperinflation, political crisis	7649	92
Venezuela	1989	Political crisis, inflation	81	61
Non reformers				
Dominican Republic				
Ecuador				
Haiti				

* Year reforms started. Dx/GDP = Foreign debt/Gross Domestic Product.
Source: Author's table based on data from Sebastian Edwards.

This model for the political economies of the region was adopted as the new paradigm first in Bolivia (August 1985), then in Mexico (July 1988), Venezuela (February 1989), Argentina (July 1989), and Peru (July 1990) and eventually was assimilated, either by imitation, contagion, or necessity, by the smaller countries (Uruguay in March 1990 and Paraguay in August 1993, although to a lesser degree). It finally reached Brazil in July of 1994, Ecuador in 1995, and Central American countries between 1992 and 1995.[169]

The matrix developed by Ramón Frediani and shown in Table 6-3 and 6-4 clearly shows a group of countries, among them Argentina, Chile, and Peru, where the reforms appear to be in a later stage. A second group includes Bolivia, Mexico, and Brazil, and in a third group of countries the reforms are fragmentary and nascent, such as Uruguay and Venezuela.

TABLE 6-3
Performance of Structural Reforms

Country	Privatizations	Reform of the State	Reduction of Trade Barriers	Deregulation of Domestic Markets
Argentina	3	2	3	3
Bolivia	1	1	3	2
Brazil	1	1	1	1
Chile	4	3	4	4
Mexico	3	2	2	2
Peru	3	2	2	2
Uruguay	1	1	2	1
Venezuela	1	1	2	1

Note: 0: Policies are not under way or are in planning stage; 1: initial stage; 2: intermediate stage; 3: advanced stage; 4: process completed.
Source: Ramón O. Frediani, Planes de estabilización y reforma estructural en América latina, Centro Interdisciplinario de Estudios sobre el Desarrollo Latinoamericano (CIEDLA), Fundación Konrad Adenauer, Buenos Aires, 1995.

TABLE 6-4
Price Stability and Monetary and Financial Situation

Country	Price Stability	Central Bank Independence	International Reserves	Banking Reform
Argentina	4	4	3	2
Bolivia	3	3	2	3
Brazil	2	1	3	1
Chile	3	4	4	4
Mexico	1	1	2	2
Peru	3	3	3	3
Uruguay	0	1	2	2
Venezuela	0	1	2	2

Note: 0: Policies are not under way or are in planning stage; 1: initial stage; 2: intermediate stage; 3: advanced stage; 4: process completed.
Source: Ramón O. Frediani, Planes de estabilización y reforma estructural en América latina, Centro Interdisciplinario de Estudios sobre el Desarrollo Latinoamericano (CIEDLA), Fundación Konrad Adenauer, Buenos Aires, 1995.

Table 6-5
Evolution of Economic Freedom Index for Selected Latin American Countries
(maximum possible value is 10, minimum 0)

Country	1975	1993–1995	2002	Ranking 2002	Is Economic Freedom Higher for the Period?
Argentina	3.1	6.3	5,8	86	Yes (+ 2,7)
Bolivia	5.5	6.4	6,5	58	No relevant change (+ 1.0)
Brazil	3.2	3.3	6,2	74	Yes (+ 3.0)
Chile	2.8	5.8	7,3	22	Yes (+ 4.5)
Colombia	4.3	5.3	4,9	107	No relevant change (0,6)
Costa Rica	5.2	6.7	7,1	31	Yes (+ 1.9)
Dominican Rep	3.6	5.7	6,6	51	Yes (+ 3.0)
Ecuador	4.3	5.9	5,6	94	Yes (+ 1.3)
El Salvador	4.7	6.3	7,2	27	Yes (+ 2,5)
Guatemala	6.5	6.5	6,4	61	No relevant change (-0,1)
Honduras	7.4	5.5	6,4	61	No (- 1.0)
Mexico	5.0	5.8	6,5	58	No relevant change (+ 1,0)
Nicaragua	6.4	3.3	6,4	61	No (0,0)
Panama	7.0	6.6	7,2	27	No relevant change (+ 0,2)
Paraguay	5.6	6.1	6,2	74	No relevant change (+ 0.6)
Peru	3.7	5.9	6,8	44	Yes (+ 3.1)
Uruguay	5.8	6.1	6,8	44	No relevant change (+ 1.0)
Venezuela	6.9	4.5	4,6	118	No (- 2.3)

Source: Author's table, with data from Economic Freedom of the World (1975–1995), Fraser Institute. The index used is the summary index (Is1) of economic freedom. Economic Freedom of the World (2004), Fraser Institute.

A closer analysis of the economic reforms yields repeated pro-market references, to terms such as privatization, deregulation, and economic openness. While the use of the terms points to a healthy intention to clear and simplify markets, if not done properly, they may eventually involve rent-seeking and involuntary income redistribution.

Indicators of economic freedom help to better understand the depth and direction of the reforms. Given that economic freedom is a necessary pre-requisite for economic growth — because of the incentives it generates and the lesser number of distortions — it is relevant to find out whether the reforms have, in fact, increased economic freedom. The Index of Economic Freedom, developed by the Canadian Fraser Institute, measures economic freedom among nations utilizing objective information that can be updated regularly.[170]

The most relevant countries in the region — Brazil, Mexico, and Venezuela — did not experience improvements in economic freedom for the period 1975 to 1993/95 — the first two remained unchanged, while in the latter, conditions worsened. Argentina (+ 3.3), Chile (+ 3), and Peru (+ 2.2) have improved the most in terms of economic freedom. Among 102 countries measured for economic freedom, Brazil ranks 93rd and Venezuela 63rd.

The Rent-Seeking Character of the Reforms

The policies implemented to solve the problems faced by the different countries (privatization, openness, deregulation, and reform of the state) had multiple, and sometimes incompatible, objectives. At the same time, attempts were made to solve the root causes (inflation, in particular), improve allocation of scarce resources, distribute private rents, and strengthen public finances.

In many cases, the countries pursued contradictory economic policy goals. For example, the larger goal of efficient resource allocation was lost when privatizations were undertaken in order to provide revenue for the state. Such was the case in the sale of state-owned telephone corporations in Argentina and Brazil to private corporations along with monopoly rights for a number of years.

The privatization process included many areas in which national states had been involved: telephones, airlines, railroads, electricity, ports, maritime transport, roads, television and radio, permits for oil and gas exploitation, meat processing, military manufacturing, among others. The spirit behind the privatization program, however, was one of contracting out rather than the final sale of assets to the private sector. A report by Argentina's Secretariat of Economic Planning stated the following:

> The process of transferring public assets to the private sector is not a mere transfer of a set of assets to be freely disposed of. What is essentially transferred is the concession to apply the specific set of assets to the

provision of specific goods and/or services to a specific potential market, for a definite period of time. Thus, an adequate estimate of the expected income flows and a regulatory environment that contemplates rates and service provision are the necessary framework to ensure the continuity of the public utility under efficient and equitable conditions.[171]

This is what the government understood as "privatization." First, the state assets were sold without deregulating the corresponding markets, and monopoly rights were granted for a period of time. Second, the buyers were not free to dispose of the transferred assets. Rather, regulations were put in place to describe not only the uses to which the assets could be assigned, but also the shape of the market, the rate levels for utilities, the quality of the services to be provided, etc. The privatization process, especially for public utilities, became largely a mechanism for enhancing fiscal revenue. Publicly owned corporations were transferred to private monopolies.

These private monopolists were the net winners, gaining concentrated negotiating power through the control of the former state corporation. The state, in turn, commands a higher price than it would if it deregulated the market and transferred the assets into a competitive situation. By allocating the proceeds from the asset sales to reducing the fiscal deficit, the country's risk is reduced and foreign investments are attracted. What is not seen here is that resources could be allocated more efficiently under competitive and open rules. Aaron Tornell explains,

> The Mexican experience raises the question of why the reforms were implemented at a time of economic crisis rather than at a time of bonanza, when the country might have been able to "afford" the short term costs more easily. One may look at this puzzle in at least two ways. A first perspective would be that the government had the latitude to act as if it were a central planner who maximizes some objective function and does not face any pressure from interest groups. According to this view, in the Mexican case, presidents Echeverria (1970–76) and Lopez Portillo (1976–82) either did what they deemed best, or what was in fashion throughout the world at that particular time, while Presidents de la Madrid (1982–88) and Salinas (1988–94) decided to follow the reformist vogue of the eighties.... By contrast, the second view would be that governments do no act in a vacuum, but in a jungle of rent-seeking groups. In this view, economic policy ceases to be the design of the central planner and becomes the result of interaction between rent seeking groups. Thus, in order to understand changes in economic policy, we would have to analyze the gains and losses of each interest group. In all likelihood, the correct explanation is a combination of both these perspectives.[172]

A similar argument helps explain the origin of the reforms in Chile during the 1970s:

> Unlike Mexico, in Chile it was not a drastic Collapse in terms of trade that induced the breakdown of the status quo, but rather "the arrival of several new guests at the dinner table of the distributive state" in the sixties. Among them were the traditional urban labor movement, the shantytown dwellers, and rural labor. However, the effect, was the same as in Mexico: less available fiscal revenue for each group. This increased the incentives to incur the short-run costs necessary to eliminate the power of the other groups. The results were the wave of expropriations and strikes of 1970–73 and the trade liberalization of 1975. As established interest groups weakened one another, Pinochet acquired autonomy to act as he saw fit.[173]

Features Shared by Latin American Reforms

The economic reforms in Latin American countries shared common instruments such as privatization, tariff reform, and public sector reforms, but they also shared features that deserve an in-depth look:

Motivating Factors or Catalysts

External shocks (foreign financing and decline of the terms of exchange) or acute domestic conditions (inflation) weakened the administrations and altered the distribution of rents. Incentives arose to allow deeper reform processes. Governments acted as benevolent planners and responded to interest group demands for rents derived from state activities.

Reforms With Fiscal and Rent Goals

Governments implemented the reforms with an eye to restoring financing sources, while interest groups with negotiating power attempted to gain as good a starting position as possible under the new rules. A tool shared by all the countries, privatization, accomplished the goals for both groups: administrations maximized rents by granting monopolistic rights, and interest groups were guaranteed captive markets, whose profitability in some cases had statutory guarantees.

State Role Unchanged

The reforms effected changes in the administrative structure of the national states but did not radically change their roles in the economy. In none of the reformist countries did the role of the state in the economy shrink substantially. Moreover, the role of the state grew as economic services (such as utilities) were replaced by social spending. Public spending continued to rise in spite of privatizations and debt reduction (under the Brady plan). In many countries, the deregulatory efforts at the national level resulted in more regulation at the lower levels of government, again showing the difficulties involved in removing public and private rents from regulation.

Use of Illegal Mechanisms

The terminal nature of the crises acted as justification for all kind of measures inconsistent with a limited state and the protection of rights. Latin American reforms are full of expropriation of bank deposits (Plan Bonex, Argentina 1990, Plan Collor, Brazil 1990) and expropriation of bank deposits and asymmetrical devaluation, Argentina 2002, wage and salary increases declared by decree (Chile 1980), nationalizations (banking crisis, Mexico 1982), and price and wage controls (Pacto Social Económico, Mexico 1987). Add to this list the institutional deviations and shortcuts that were justified for constitutional changes that hid election motives, changes in the number of Supreme Court Justices, cases of electoral fraud, the use of administrative decrees rather than statutes to legislate fundamental issues, and the dissolution of legislative bodies.

Slower Pace of the Reforms

The early steps of the reforms had a very fast pace. Privatizations attract capital, openness helps to stop price escalations, and fiscal reforms restore financing sources. However, once these steps are in place, more difficult aspects need to be addressed, which are also less public and carry higher costs in terms of losers and foregone rents. Reforms tend to come to a halt when they face the unions, the political system, the redistribution of income at the provincial level, education and health, and judicial and law enforcement systems. Reformers need votes and electoral victories, and these are harder to come by when the short-term costs (sacrificed rents) of the reforms exceed the long-term benefits (better allocation of resources).

Public Spending: the Root of All Distortions

An important feature of the Latin American reform processes is that they have been accompanied by continuous increases in public spending.

In general, initial higher revenues are directly transferred to public spending, which tends to go up. In effect, politicians are acting like maximizing entrepreneurs, and as such have the incentive to spend more as their revenues keep rising.

For decades, analysts focused on the evils of financing the fiscal deficit through monetary emission. Money injected into the market was not absorbed by the public's demand, which resulted in higher prices. It was generally agreed that inflation was not only the biggest economic problem in Latin America, but the only one. The only discussion was about the magnitude of the deficit and its financing.

Few warned about the magnitude of public spending. Yet, recent research suggests that the amount of public spending is not neutral, and, regardless of its financing source, it generates relevant disequilibriums. In fact, even if the fiscal deficit were zero, a high level of public spending brings about imbalances in the balance of payments and distortions in the productive system.[174]

Armando Ribas explains that "in the long term, there is a larger problem in the relationship between State and market. Public spending alters this relationship; the State is not only *not* part of the Product, it is one of its most significant costs. In other words, the higher public spending, and the lesser its efficiency, the lesser the productivity of the non-public productive sector. The level of public spending determines the efficiency of the economy as a whole.... For better or worse, production is not a given; there will be more or less wealth created depending on whether the State decides to redistribute it. We can then say that after a threshold of public spending, the figure for wealth creation can become negative."[175]

The growth in public spending observed during the last decade distorts the productive sector. Public spending increases consumption demand, raising the price of services (which cannot be imported), and even wages, while the increase in imports competes with domestic products, at lower prices (due to the fixed exchange rate) and with lower tariffs.

Companies started having profitability problems: on the one hand they could not raise their prices due to foreign competition. On the other, the interest rates were going up because part of the savings were being used to finance public spending. These distortions eventually led to problems such as hyperinflation, the very problems the reforms sought to eradicate. The "tequila effect" and the 1998–99 crisis in Brazil are examples of this.[176] There is a fundamental relationship that helps explain the origin of these imbalances: when the real interest rate is higher than the rate of profitability, it generates a trade imbalance (exports minus imports).

Armando Ribas and Eliot Kalter analyzed the case of Mexico in 1994.

The fiscal deficit had surprised analysts and declined by 15 percent of GDP in 1987, to a level under 1 percent during 1992–93. It was not the deficit that caused the Mexican debacle and the collapse of the peso (devalued by 70 percent). However, public spending was growing at the same rate as fiscal revenues. At one point, the increase in the cost of goods became untenable, and the deficit could no longer be financed through trade. The political inability to reduce spending led to an exchange rate crisis that became known as the "tequila effect."[177]

Table 6-6 shows growth both in spending and debt during the 1990s, reminding us that the reforms were weak and would eventually lead to more trouble. It shows that participation of the public sector in the GDP remained constant, and actually grew in real terms.

The table shows the evolution of public spending during the 1990s. In spite of the reforms allegedly aimed at promoting a market economy, public expenditure went up in selected countries. In the case of Argentina, Brazil, Mexico and Venezuela levels are higher than prior to the reforms. In the 1990s, GDP grew by 54 percent in Argentina, 17 percent in Brazil, 28 percent in Mexico, and 32 percent in Venezuela. Public spending in real terms increased and shows the larger role of the public sector in spite of attempts at reform. The economic reforms did not reduce public spending. Paradoxically, the privatization and deregulation plan did not reduce the state's intervention in the economy.

TABLE 6-6
Participation of the State in the Economy and Growth of GDP for Selected Countries

Year	Argentina		Brazil		Venezuela		Mexico	
	Public Spending/GDP	GDP Change	Public Spending/GDP	GDP Change	Public Spending/GDP	GDP Change	Public Spending/GDP	GDP Change
1990	28.6	-1.8	33.2	-4.2	32.8	6.9	27.5	4.5
1991	28.4	10.8	30.6	0.3	33.3	9.7	23.8	3.6
1992	29.1	9.6	30.7	-0.8	30.2	6.1	22.2	2.8
1993	29.0	5.7	33.3	4.2	27.2	0.3	22.5	0.7
1994	29.1	8.0	29.3	6.0	32.1	-2.3	23.1	4.5
1995	29.9	-4.0	32.8	4.2	33.1	3.7	23.0	-6.2
1996	27.9	4.8	32.9	2.8	28.1	-0.4	23.8	5.1
1997	27.1	8.6	34.1	3.7	29.9	5.1	23.6	7.0
1998	28.5	4.2	40.2	0.2	29.9	-0.7	21.9	4.2
Var. 90–99		54.7%		17.1%		32%		28.7%

Source: ECLAC, Annual report, 1999. Figures for Argentina, Secretaría de Programación Económica, "Informe, Caracterización del gasto público social."

Institutional Change

In spite of recent progress in several countries in Latin America (Argentina, Chile, Mexico), the institutions inherited from Spain and Portugal still prevail, among them the lack of constraints on government's role in allocating economic resources; the absence of an independent Judiciary, capable of enforcing constitutional restrictions on the Executive and Legislative branches; and the uncertainty of rules that change with every administration.

The so-called Latin American economic reform left intact basic institutional aspects that were part of the welfare and business state. Even after the reforms, the governments continue to be the principal protagonists of economic life. The level of public spending on multiple functions, the large regulatory power over private activity, and the interference with contracts and prices are tools of intervention that remain unchanged years after the reforms were implemented.

The role of the Judiciary is also muddled. The intricate and suffocating maze of statutes it must apply and constant political interference conspire to make it a hurdle instead of a vigilant arm ensuring the respect for constitutional rights and agreements among private persons.

For Douglass North, institutional change is a complex process by which changes at the margin can arise from changes in rules, informal constraints, and varying degrees and observance of enforcement. In addition, he states that institutions change incrementally, rather than in a discontinuous fashion. And even though formal rules can change overnight as a result of political or judicial decisions, informal constraints, embedded in uses, traditions, and rules of behavior are much more resistant and harder to penetrate. These cultural limitations not only connect the past with present and future, but they also provide us with the key to explain the direction of historical change.[178]

According to North, institutional change takes place either through 1) the symbiotic relationship between institutions and the organizations that have evolved as a consequence of incentives or 2) the feedback process by which human beings perceive changes in the set of opportunities and react to them. Incremental change happens when entrepreneurs in political and economic organizations perceive that they could profit from altering the existing institutional framework. But, above all, perceptions depend both on the information these entrepreneurs receive and on the way they process it.[179] In Argentina, for example, upon initiating the reform process in 1989, President Carlos Menem perceived that the alteration of a relevant set of economic rules would be more profitable than the *status quo*.

Douglass North's notion of the "political entrepreneur" applies here, defining a person that takes risks that may result in gains or losses, *ex ante* lacking complete information and acts in a context of uncertainty. Along these lines are also the examples of Pinochet in Chile, Fujimori in Peru, and Goni Sánchez de Losada in Bolivia.

In recent decades, the New Political Economy has attempted to understand the behavior of governments and other agents—traditionally studied under political science—based on assumptions of rational behavior and individual utility maximization, concepts originally developed for microeconomic analysis. This has given more realism to the analysis of the processes by which public policies are developed. One of the central goals of this approach is to reveal "the fallacy of the benevolent planner." As does any other individual, the policy maker pursues his or her own interests, which do not necessarily match those of the individuals for whom he is planning. Mariano Tomassi and Sebastián Saiegh write,

> ...The assumption that a benevolent planner implements policies recommended by an economist is simplistic, wrong and even, in certain circumstances, can be dangerous; furthermore, it is inconsistent with the basic tenets of microeconomics. In many cases, governments do not adopt "socially optimal" policy recommendations because public officials rationally pursue their own interests, and these often do not coincide with the public interest.[180]

The authors that observe the economic reform process through the lens of optimism are justified in light of the growth outcomes of many countries in the region. But it is also true that this is not the first time that the Latin American economies have been open and have enjoyed reduced government interference.

Conclusion

The Latin American reforms are widely viewed as the result of neoliberal policies. No doubt, the prefix *neo* attempts to connote something new or modern, whereas the second part purports to identify classical liberalism. Neither is correct. The confusion may stem from the fact that the reforms resorted to mechanisms such as "privatization" (about which serious questions have been raised), opening of the economy (which was only partial), and the notion of denationalizing the economy (which remains incomplete). Another reason for the confusion in the use of terms is that some supporters of interventionism would like to disqualify liberalism by associating it with the current measures.

Just as the economic reform policies are not new, they are also not liberal. Liberalism describes a limited state, with specific and relatively few functions and the lowest tax levels possible; the enforcement of contracts written and entered into by private persons, not by legislators; and respect for private property and individual initiative as the engine of sustained and permanent growth. The division of powers, with three independent branches and decentralization of functions, constitute the institutional framework necessary for the principles to work. In contrast, within the Latin American reforms, governments are unlimited, with their myriad functions needing growing levels of public spending and debt.

The regulations resulting from the reforms, far from ensuring competitive conditions for public utilities and other former publicly provided services, substituted profitable private monopolies for the public monopolies.

The opening of the region's economies to international markets was closer to managed trade than to free trade. Tariffs were not reduced substantially for products coming from all countries, but rather the policy meant negotiated reductions for some countries under partner agreements, creating veritable supra-national barriers for non-members. Instead of profiting from the benefits of worldwide trade, they selected sectors to benefit from trade with poor and small nations. By limiting openness to member countries, the Latin American countries allowed industrial lobbies to strengthen their positions, sacrificing an efficient allocation of resources. Far from creating more trade opportunities and expanding competition, blocks close markets and divert trade. Mercosur, the Comunidad Andina (formerly Pacto Andino), and the endless bilateral agreements under ALADI show that the countries in the region do not intend to trade with the world but to open markets slightly without risking international competition.

Other mechanisms of involuntary income redistribution remain in place, allowing us to dispute the existence of a true liberalism, among them public pension systems, active economic development policies for selected industries, statutory privileges for powerful trade unions, and a suffocating tax system (both in terms of amount and compliance costs).

We can conclude that the Latin American reforms do not amount to a movement toward liberalism. The reforms are made up of interventionist measures, which are neither new nor respect the ideas of liberty. In 1927, Ludwig von Mises wrote that when one runs into liberals that agree to the nationalization of the railroads, mines, and other corporations, and even favor protectionist tariffs, one has to conclude that all that remains of liberalism is the name.[181] Similarly, within reforms that do not respect private property rights, impose protectionist tariffs, and maintain subsidies, the very notions of the republic and the division of powers are violated. To confuse such a state of affairs with liberalism is a complete mistake.

7
The Counter Reforms of the New Century

The Latin American Reforms and Their Feet of Clay

Just when a large part of the world thought that Latin America was fully immersed in a new era of capitalism and economic openness, profound crises took hold of the most important countries in the region. The crises revealed that the economic reforms had feet of clay, that they had been built on old institutional roots, and that they could not overcome the phenomenal opposition of traditional power groups.

The 21st century finds many Latin American countries mired in stagnating economies and politically unable to change their basic rules. In other similar historical situations swift and lasting institutional change in the region did not occur. Latin America is now divided in two areas:

- One: Central America, Chile and Mexico,
- Two: the counter reform countries Venezuela, Uruguay, Argentina, Bolivia, Peru and Ecuador where the rule of law and private property rights are being overlooked.

The two other countries remaining are Brazil with a government that originated in a left wing party and Colombia with part of the country under a guerrilla control. Both countries are unpredictable today.

The counter reform countries are perceived by economic agents as having greater risk for investments. Economic agents observe that rules change therefore their ability to predict the legal framework is limited and risk goes up. When risk goes up, profitability for investments must increase. As a result, the number of projects that are carried out has come down, and so

7. The Counter Reforms of the New Century

has investments, employment and growth. The violation of explicit and tacit agreements increases risk by reducing predictability of the future. Entrepreneurial activity is culturally depreciated, which feeds into the voracity of public officials. Public officials respond to crises with the threat that if domestic prices rise, tariffs for imports will be lowered, or export duties will increase so prices in the local market are equivalent (up to 45 percent duty for crude exports) making rules subject to the whim of whoever is in charge. Rules respond to personal agreements made by influential politicians. Politics makes the rules rather than rules providing a framework for politics. Business transactions depend on volatile rules subject to frequent changes.

Respect for the law, then, is weak. Congress members seem to think they can change everything. A member of Congress in Argentina recently told a reporter, "We can change everything except the law of gravity." Officials aim for what they consider to be good for society rather than applying the law that would give society legal guarantees (Rawls).

With rules being so unpredictable, what is predictable is a bleak future unless some basic changes are made. Investment will drop abruptly, and so will the entrepreneurial business climate and consequently, employment and prospects for progress. In such a scenario, distributive tendencies and struggles among the different sectors of society will become atrocious. The result of these struggles will be an economy closed to trade, blocked in its domestic activity, and with it a steep rise in poverty.

New attempts at radical change will only become possible in the context of a terminal and even explosive crisis. In these conditions, where one cannot distribute what does not exist and where the losers of a failed model face the winners of another failed model, any attempt to propose a consistent, creative solution will fail.

The reforms in these countries have slowed down or come to a halt, rent-seeking institutions have prevailed over change opportunities, when pressure groups closed ranks and became stronger to stop the forces of change. Argentina has now devalued its currency and defaulted on its public debt. Ecuador did the same in 2000, Chávez in Venezuela, devalued in January 2002 and increased state intervention supported by high oil revenues cramping down on freedom of speech and individual liberties.

In the other America: Central America, Chile and Mexico where the reforms advanced, a positive dynamic force has developed, supported by external factors, such as a profound integration of trade and international investments in the first case, and in the second, the historic trade partnership through NAFTA of an underdeveloped Latin American country with two developed Anglo-Saxon nations—Canada and the United States with Chile being the next in line.

I Venezuela: High Oil Prices Allow Dreams of Castro

For Venezuela, the arrival of Hugo Chávez launched an era of anachronistic populism more consistent with the post–World War II period than with the beginnings of the 21st century, with his "banana republic" attitude and his messianic return in April 2002.

Many analysts see this so-called Bolivar revolution as nothing but an attempt to Cubanize the economy, that is, the adoption of a communist economic regime with strong State intervention and serious limitations to private property rights. According to economist Alexander Guerrero, a researcher at CEDICE, statutory limitations imposed on property rights have transformed them, placing severe limitations on private investment given the monopoly of the State in areas of the economy where private investment would be more efficient and profitable. Land reform shows the ideological roots of the Cuban model, where private property rights on land are completely absent as they are in oil and gas, the seashore, fishing, transport, and other restricted sectors. Moreover, the declaration of social interest hides its communist roots, weakening property rights, production, markets, value creation, and the freedom to choose and work.

Chavez' single mode state can only survive due to high oil prices and big resources, which are publicly owned and which represent more than 60 percent of public revenues. Guerrero, in his paper "Todo el Petróleo para el fisco" uses the phrase "from the well to the public coffers" referring to the role of oil in Venezuelan public finances, implemented through a regime of public rights of the subsurface and an oil industry nationalized since 1975.

The weakest point of the economy is that it is based on high international prices for crude and is highly dependent on this volatile price. A big drop in the international price will put the administration in a serious crisis, which means the devaluation of the bolívar threatening the ability of the state to borrow.

Venezuela is the country in the region least inclined to reforming its institutions. The almost free financing that oil provides may be its biggest enemy. Paradoxically, oil is stopping the country from undertaking institutional changes that will transform rent-seeking vices into productive habits. Economic prosperity in some years can almost exclusively be attributed to oil prices, as economic growth statistics show. Data from ECLAC 2001 show that in the last 10 years, Venezuela had the greatest variability in terms of GDP growth. It had five years (1991, 92, 95, 97, and 2000) of positive economic growth at rates above 4 percent, while for the other five years, figures show deep recession with negative GDP rates (1993, 94, 96, 98, and 99).

Venezuela is at the mercy of crude oil prices that it does not control.

II Argentina: Reforms of the 90's Washed Away

What Argentina undertook in the 1990s can hardly be defined as real economic reforms, but was rather a fiscalist response to a terminal situation. The current Argentine crisis (detailed in chapter 8) reveals what may be the most important lesson about these processes: changes that do not affect basic institutions are weak, transitory, and explosive. The hyperinflation of 1989 was the culmination of five decades of political errors in the short term and a clear bent toward a rent-seeking culture in the long term. The main components of this were a closed economy, a state financed through currency printing, distributive struggles as the basis for price setting, public employment, and growing public spending.

The reforms begun in 1989 by the administration of Carlos Menem were as initially surprising as they were appealing. International analysts, statesmen, bankers, and investors around the world considered Argentina the end-of-the-century miracle, the example to follow, the star of the emerging markets. If the measures implemented were appealing at first, it was not for their essence but for the contrast they provided with the previous decade. Argentines were delighted to have reliable telephone service, enjoy electric power in the summer and gas in the winter, see that their salaries held their value day after day, have access to ten-year loans, have a stable currency, etc. That appeal was reflected in the votes that gave Menem his second term in office.

These reforms were advertised as relatively successful especially when they afforded some stability during crises elsewhere in the world. However, the government still had a chronic primary deficit that was financed in the early years by the sale of state-owned utilities, which brought in close to $30 billion, and later on, by public debt to the tune of $65 billion. At the same time, tax collections were rising to an average of about $30 billion annually between 1990 and 2000. These higher revenues increased consumer demand strongly, which led to real GDP growth of 35 percent between 1990 and 1996. At the same time, the higher borrowing from the State raised dollar interest rates for domestic companies, which paid real interest rates of up to 15 and 20 percent. This state of affairs, together with the growing tax burden and a peso anchored to the dollar, meant that domestic tradable goods were no longer competitive relative to imported ones. Reforming institutions to allow for legal stability, respect for the property rights, liberty and a competitive environment was not discussed or even considered seriously by administration officials or economic policy makers—much less by national or provincial legislators.

When Fernando de la Rúa took office as President in 2000, another opportunity was quickly wasted. Not only were no efforts made to reduce public spending—the source of all evils—but the cosmetic reforms of the 1990s were abandoned. The high foreign debt (US$ 135 billion), the destruction of local industry, and the potential bankrupt banking system due to loans to the State finally destroyed this economy of privileges and favoritisms.

The explosion of 2001 was due to the inability of the government to continue financing their expenditures with domestic or foreign public debt. The first symptom was the confiscation of deposits followed by default on the public debt held by local and foreign creditors, a 70 percent devaluation of the currency and the postponement of private sector contracts and obligations such as mortgage payments for a period of over two years.

After a GDP drop of 20 percent, the economy has recovered in the last three years thanks to import substitution (due to devaluation) and high prices for agriculture commodities and oil. Nevertheless, we believe the trend will be more government control (take over of public utilities) and greater closing of the economy.

III Uruguay: Modifying Behavior of State Ownership

Tabaré Vazquez who won the last election demonstrated that the public is willing to keep publicly owned corporations unchanged, just as they were when created in the 1950s. Delivery of utilities (gas, water, electricity, and telephone services), the production of oil, and the distribution of cement and other raw materials is carried out by state companies. And if votes are a measure of popular support, these are widely popular.

Nevertheless, Uruguay is a relatively orderly country, which for decades has maintained manageable deficit levels, moderate inflation rates, and higher growth rates than the average for the region. In the context of countries with unstable banking regulation, although they suffered severely Argentina's collapse, they showed respect for private property rights. Uruguay's decades-long respect for financial activities affords it comparative advantages in banking services.

So in spite of its tradition of respect for private property rights, President Tabaré Vazquez is moving towards greater intervention of the State in the economy. It will be interesting to see whether sensible political will can overcome the behaviour of State owned enterprises and heavy intervention in the economy. This is in line with what their neighbors Argentina and Bolivia are backsliding into the past.

IV Bolivia: Zero Sum Game

The growth of the economy during the 90's was about 4 percent per annum. During the last four years the government implemented a project of eliminating growth of cocaine: it had a severe negative impact on the economy. The previous two presidents believed they could replace unofficial cocaine exports with gas sales to Brazil and Argentina but the last president Mesa was pushed from power by a strong Indian population *which* took over the streets demanding nationalization of all resources and strong state regulation of the economy. Protection of private property and contracts have not been honored.

V Ecuador: Moving Against Reforms of the 90's

In 1999, Ecuador's economy dropped by 9.5 percent, a figure comparable to the notorious 8 percent collapse of production in the United States in 1931. At the end of that year, with unemployment close to 16 percent, the IMF began to pressure Ecuador to raise the VAT from 10 percent to 15 percent. The final increase agreed to was 12 percent (after a surcharge on import duties). As could have been predicted, this made a bad situation worse, similar to the effect of raising the VAT in Japan in 1998. Moreover, in an effort to placate the IMF, the corporate income tax rate was raised from 15 percent to 25 percent; still, in an economy that had shrunk by almost 10 percent not many businesses were reporting taxable incomes.

With the currency in dire straits, and the imposition of new taxes on a banking system in crisis, capital flight reached an astounding 19 percent of GDP in 1999, forcing imports down to half.

In 2000, in the face of the crisis and the proven inability of the country's leaders to propose responsible monetary policy, Ecuador allowed the circulation, transactions and agreements to be made both in sucres and in US dollars, thus taking away from the government the unlimited ability to finance itself through the inflationary tax.

But merely adopting a bold monetary scheme does not constitute profound institutional change. Dollarization is a just step; at best, it may turn out to be a constraint sufficient to force the political system to initiate serious change. But as a tool it is insufficient.

Figures for the year 2000 show that the 1999 drop was reverted, and preliminary numbers for 2001 reinforce the growth trends.[182] Notwithstanding this, Ecuador still needs reform of the public sector, lower trade barriers, and strong judicial respect for private agreements. A report by the U.S. State Department states that "in practice the Judiciary continues to be slow and inconsistent. It has been reported that judges accelerate or delay their decisions induced by political pressure or the payment of bribes."[183] Obstacles to business, the weak observance of property rights, and price controls on certain goods are evidence that institutional reforms are lacking. This reflects a great political instability where the rule of law is lacking.

VI Brazil: Potential Explosion of a Public Debt Bomb

Brazil is enjoying the benefits of the early stages of economic reforms. Telephone privatization and an incipient opening of the oil business do not constitute radical, substantial change, but they have afforded the country a generous dose of revenue that has found positive response both with the general public and with investors.

Brazil is only in its fifth year of low inflation, after seeing hyperinflationary levels in the early 1990s. In 2004, GDP grew less 1 percent, while the unemployment rate is at 7 percent.

These economic indicators fail to reflect institutional inadequacies. Brazil continues to be one of the world's most closed economies, with levels of regulation and cross-subsidies that transform productive activity into a game of business lobbying. According to the Heritage Foundation, "Economic development remains thwarted by illiquid and overregulated markets that attract little capital, as well as a convoluted and punitive tax code."[184]

While Mexico's exports tripled between 1992 and 2000 (thanks to NAFTA), Brazilian exports for the same period grew 61 percent—a performance lower than Chile's, whose exports grew by 78 percent.

Brazil will be able to maintain a "market friendly attitude" as long as its large domestic market (although with low real incomes) allows it to finance the inefficiencies associated with protectionism and the public sector. Unfortunately, the hyperinflation of the 1990s seems not to have spurred serious reforms. A lesson from the Brazilian case is that in these economies with such deeply rooted institutional traditions, the existence of financing proves to be an obstacle for true reform. The financing packages that Brazil keeps receiving from international agencies, together with high devaluation rates, allow the country to continue financing the disequilibriums resulting from its closed institutions.

The public debt grew in eight years from US$ 60 billion in 1994 to US$ 370 billion by March 2002. The PT (Workers Party) that won the election in 2002 continue to finance government expenditure with foreign investment (US$ 9.800 million) public debts and taxes and thus increasing the explosion of the public spending time bomb.

VII Colombia: Civil War with Drug Lords

Colombia suffers three mayor threats: drugs, terrorism (FARC / ELN) and criminality. According to the local authorities cocaine eradication is down 50 percent since the government of Uribe came to power. Notwithstanding, GNP increase about 2 percent and the unemployment dropped 13 percent in 2003. The principal exports are crude and coffee which allowed Colombia to have historic level of exports reaching $18.000 million. Notwithstanding this, the protection of private property is still poor due to intimidation carried out in the lower courts. We see the trend of continued government intervention in the economy and the threat of criminal activities in the future.

VIII Chile: Continuity and Depth of Reforms as a Competitive Advantage

In contrast to the examples above, in Chile and Mexico the forces in favor of institutional change seem to have prevailed over those opposed to it. The weakening of traditional power groups that thrived on the old rules of the game can be explained largely in terms of the dynamic generated by external factors and the standing of the "new winners" in light of the new policies.

Two features have been key to the success of the Chilean reforms: trade openness, which literally opened the economy to the world, and the reform of the pensions and retirement system, which made owners of the country's workers.

Chile dismantled the quota system and other barriers to trade and adopted a single tariff policy. In 1979 the tariff was set at 10 percent for all products; it currently stands at 8 percent, and it is expected to be lowered to 6 percent by 2006. José Piñera, the former Social Security Minister who implemented the innovative system of Administradoras de Fondos de Pensión (AFP), established a revolutionary pensions system of personal capitalization. It is important to note the connection between the free trade strategy and personal capitalization system. In most countries around the world, lowering trade barriers is presented as a battle between capitalists and workers, or between global elites and the ordinary man. But Chile showed that individual savings accounts invested in the market made a capitalist out of every worker, who would then have an explicit interest in an internationally competitive economy.

Piñera suggests that most Chileans benefit from free trade, not only as consumers but also as owners of the productive resources of the economy because they own retirement savings accounts. Free trade is good for the economy, and what is good for the economy is good for investors. A virtuous circle of free trade is thus established, and it has thrived independently of who holds power. During four different administrations, economic growth has averaged 7 percent annually, with exports representing 40 percent of GDP.

The Chilean case offers an important lesson. Although not a guarantee of success, trade openness poses an obstacle to pressures from those who benefit from colonial institutions. Opening the economy means finding a ceiling for prices, which acts to limit sectorial struggles that — through the printing of currency — tend to leave the consumer footing the bill. Chile developed relationships with other regions in the world, and those bonds keep getting stronger. Chile is part of APEC (a trade agreement signed by Asian countries, the United States, Mexico, Australia, and New Zealand) and has joined NAFTA. These agreements translate into growing trade with other member countries.

Local pressure groups lose power and economic policy gains a powerful tool for combating limitations on liberty set by traditional Latin institutions. This new tool, combined with the presence of new international players (that are attracted to the defense of property rights, legal guarantees and monetary stability), reduce the power of the state's former courtesans (and this is truer for Mexico than for Chile).

Chile continues to be the star of the region. Some institutional indicators speak for themselves. Over the almost 30 years since the reforms begun in 1973, continuity in government by constitutional presidents of different parties reinforces the long-term outlook that makes the rules of the game certain and guarantees the rule of law.[185] In the most recent edition of the Economic Freedom Index published by the Heritage Foundation, Chile obtains the highest score for the region in terms of economic freedom. It is the only Latin American country ranked as "free" in economic terms, together with 15 other countries out of 160 surveyed.[186]

The existence of certain protected farm sectors and leftover attempts at a producer state — represented by state-owned mining and oil companies — indicate that the reforms are not finished and that more progress needs to be made.

IX Mexico: Political Change Powered by External Factors

The other exception to the Latin American rule is Mexico, which in 1994 joined the free trade agreement that Canada and the U.S. had entered into in 1989 and would thereafter be known as NAFTA. This agreement, a rarity between developed and developing countries created strong opposition in the signing countries. Unions in the United States were concerned that investments would move to Mexico, with its cheaper labor and looser environmental laws. Supporters of the treaty united under the motto "Export goods not people" and their belief that NAFTA would spur economic growth in Mexico, which in turn would stop immigration toward the United States.

The outcome of this partnership has been astounding. Trade between the two countries has grown at an average 16 percent annually. Mexico exports 88 percent to USA and imports 62 percent from USA with a balance of payments of US$ 163 billion in 2004.

A similar situation has occurred with Canada. Mexico has consolidated its position as the second commercial partner of the United States and the first partner of Canada in Latin America. Mexico's foreign trade levels (exports plus imports) have been impressive reaching $350 billion (seven times the figure for Argentina), and the country now ranks eighth in the world in that trade category.

Since 1996, two years after the tequila crisis, Mexico has been showing sustained growth. NAFTA has not only been an economic success but has influenced the political arenas as well. In 2000, the 71-year monopoly held by the Partido Revolucionario Institucional (PRI) was broken with the victory of current president Vicente Fox. It is the first time in the history of the country that no single party holds an absolute majority in Congress; it is the country's first experience with full democracy. Consolidating changes at a time where the governing party is not as strong might prove to be an opportunity for deeper change. This is the real test for the future of Mexico.

Institutionally, NAFTA has generated such a powerful growth dynamic that it has weakened traditional power groups and opened doors to changes in the rules of the game. Today's winners in a more open Mexico are acquiring the strength to maintain and deepen the conditions. And it would hardly have been possible for Mexico to achieve such competitive openness on its own, given the power of groups opposed to change.

Still, regulations persist that reflect the need to deepen the reforms—from price controls on medicines, energy, and public utilities to the existence of productive monsters like Pemex, Cemex and other publicly owned companies that have a strong and sometimes monopolistic presence in economic activities.

X *The Crucial Role of the United States in Latin America*

In these days when the progress made in Latin America toward market economies is seriously in danger, it is worth noting that the United States has a crucial role to play. The direction of the process toward healthier economic institutions hinges on its actions or inaction.

There are two main areas where the US could help: trade and (denying) financial aid. In the case of trade, an aggressive promotion of bilateral free trade agreements might have important effects on the rules of the game. The United States has taken too long to approve the fast track—known under the Bush administration "Trade Promotion Authority" (TPA)—, to negotiate both the FTAA and free trade agreements with Chile, and to consider the recent proposal from Central America. This delay or indifference from the United States toward Latin America represents a waste of valuable opportunities to support change in the region and avoid flagrant relapses.

In light of the fiscal disarray in Latin American countries, it is imperative to limit international aid to countries in crisis, especially aid from the IMF. Systematic aid to the region only perpetuates the institutional barbarity of unlimited government spending financed by borrowing. Argentina's current crisis speaks for itself.

Paul O'Neill, former Treasury Secretary of the United States, summed up his position when he stated that the tax revenues from American plumbers should not be sent to countries that cannot solve their own problems. This might mean a turning point in the policies of that country toward crises in Latin America and even appears to be reflected in new IMF policies.

In brief, the United States can help Latin American countries not financially, since aid only finances bureaucracies and delays any chance of real change, but rather, by playing an active role in promoting trade agreements to redirect the economies of the region toward productive and competitive activities, which will eventually erode traditional power groups, the biggest enemies of change who thrive on a closed economy.

8
Argentina: One Way Trip to Collapse

Fiscal Insolvency as a Trigger

The world was taken aback by the collapse of the Argentine economy toward the end of 2001 and early 2002; in 1998 at the annual meeting of the IMF the country had been hailed as a rising star. But today, four years of recession have turned into a full-blown economic depression, and the country's population seems resigned to decreasing economic activity, unemployment of 22 percent and growing, the absence of credit and risk investment, within the context of a fragile social peace.

The reforms of the 1990s showed their feet of clay when the sources for financing Argentina's chronic fiscal deficits finally ran out. In the none of the previous 25 years, had the consolidated public sector (national State+provinces+municipalities) ever had a fiscal surplus. Even in good years when revenues skyrocketed, public spending grew at an even faster pace. For the period 1991–2000, when GDP grew by 49 percent, consolidated spending (national State+provinces+municipalities) increased by 90 percent.

During the last two decades, the Argentine State exhibited a Darwinian ability to survive and grow, and, as this chapter will show, has developed the mechanisms to free itself from the limitations the citizenship attempts to impose on its growth. The Argentine State has proved itself to be a monster that needs to live off the most productive citizens in order to survive. And it does.

The country's fiscal insolvency was clearly the result of public spending, which was inelastic at the bottom, but flexible when it came to going up. In the last two decades, the gap between revenues and expenses had always been closed thanks to the perverse ingenuity of public officials. Up until 1989 the deficit was financed through issuing currency without genuine backing, which ended up in a dramatic hyperinflationary crisis that reached the annual rate of 5,000 percent for that year. But the Convertibility Law passed in 1991 established that every peso issued had to be backed by a dollar in reserves. So the government had to look elsewhere for financing its expenses. The selling of publicly owned corporations under monopolistic conditions would provide the highest revenue possible, and for the period 1991–95 such sales yielded 30 billion dollars. When the privatizations were completed in 1995, the government turned to indebtedness, both foreign and domestic. But loans became unavailable in mid–2001 with the prospect of debt default. For the decade 1991–2001, the public debt practically doubled in size.

Financing a Voracious State

	Primary Deficit	*Source of State Financing*	*Consequence*
1983–1989	Yes	Currency issue (austral) without backing	5000% annual hyperinflation
1989–1995	Yes	Sale of state owned corporations with captive markets	Growing public spending and captive consumers
1995–2001	Yes	Indebtedness	The debt grows from 65 to 132 billion.
2001	Yes	Bonds issued without backing Default	Increase indebtness by 45%.
2003-to date	No	Export retentions on grains and oil	Increase taxation to most competitive sectors to maintain 20% unemployment
2005	No	Agreement default debt	New bonds paid 30% of default debt

Mario Teijeiro,[187] economist and President of Centro de Estudios Públicos, writes that the IMF was complicit in the incomplete reforms of that decade. Fiscal policy remains the worst mistake made at this time. In 1991, the public debt amounted to $60 billion dollars. And it could have been reduced to $35 billion if the proceeds from privatizations had been applied to debt repayment. Instead, a decidedly Keynesian policy was adopted, and in the early years of Convertibility, public spending grew almost 100 percent. When revenues from privatizations stopped trickling in, public spending levels were maintained with foreign borrowing. And even when the increase in the debt meant that interest owed grew exponentially, there was no attempt to reduce spending and the Administration turned instead to repeated tax increases. When foreign credit was exhausted in 1998, still, public spending was not reduced. Instead, domestic credit was targeted, thus reducing the stock available for the private markets, which got the recession spiral going. Finally, public spending did not go down even when domestic credit was exhausted and the prospect of default was at hand.

The story from then on, is well known. Last ditch efforts were made to avoid the unavoidable, a fate carved by administration after administration. It was only a matter of time until it all imploded under the insolvency of the public sector.

Argentina declared the largest default in history for 132 billion dollars in Christmas of 2001, the abandonment of over ten years of a peso that was 1 to 1 with the dollar, a messy devaluation and the conversion of dollar debts into pesos (which to date have lost over 70 percent of their value). This combination had destructive effects on contracts, property rights, the law, and commercial transactions in Argentina.

Forgive Us Our Debts: The Road to Default

> *As a consequence of this, our foreign trade obligations will be sacred, and I will omit no effort or sacrifice to preserve our credit, both locally and internationally, servicing our debts religiously, because I understand that the national honor depends on our full observation of this obligation* — President Julio A. Roca, October 12, 1880

Investors who intended to participate in the so-called Argentine miracle instead ended up financing the voracious Argentine State. As the graphic below shows, in the period 1991–2000 public debt doubled from 65 billion dollars to 132 billion. As the debt stock grew and economic activity dropped, the recession consolidated, and, as the risk of lending to the Argentine government kept growing so did the interest rates that it was forced to pay. As drug addicts do, the government required an increasing dose of indebtedness to be satisfied. But unlike addicts, the government did not feel the pinch of its spending; rather, the burden fell on an increasingly impoverished population.

Mario Teijeiro[188] argues that the formula of higher public spending combined with external financing created a boom in the early stages of

Convertibility. But it eventually condemned Convertibility to failure in the medium term with the explosive public debt that was accumulating.

A growth strategy based on borrowing—be it for a government, a family or a business—is a dangerous one that can act as a boomerang in the medium term. Borrowing can make sense when it is done at low levels, paying low interest rates, and the loan is applied to a profitable investment. But it may turn catastrophic when the debt is foreign, rates paid are high, and the loan is applied to consumption or investment in noncommercial areas. Unfortunately, this is what happened in Argentina during the last decade. The family jewels were sold and too much money was borrowed, in order to first increase and then maintain unproductive public spending at untenable levels. In the case of private investment, loans were largely allocated to highways, shopping malls, and privatized utilities. Contracting a debt denominated in dollars for the purpose of consuming or investing in sectors that neither generate nor save income is an explosive formula the consequences of which are evident in the public and private defaults.

It also brought about a lag in the terms of exchange with perverse consequences for the productive structure. Inflation and domestic costs continued to grow long after Convertibility was implemented, although indexing clauses were eliminated from contracts. The exchange lag was explained by growth in public and private spending, financed through foreign debt. Teijeiro adds that the root of our problems was in the beginning of Convertibility, "those golden years nobody dares criticize."

In 1995 the Argentine government resorted to selling public bonds to foreign investors, who by 1998 were starting to doubt they would ever get their money back. So it had to turn to domestic credit, in a strange combination of voluntary credit and involuntary politically negotiated credit from domestic banks and retirement funds or Administradoras de Fondos de Jubilaciones y Pensiones (AFJP). The public sector's foray into capital markets siphoned the diminishing credit available, crowding out the private market.

In July 2001, in the face of the lack of voluntary credit from local bank depositors, the administration announced a zero-deficit policy, which was more a reflection of the "zero credit" attitude of creditors. This zero-deficit policy really amounted to the obligation on the part of the State to finance itself through tax revenues, and so far the goal has not been met. For the weak administration of Fernando de la Rua, it became increasingly difficult to tackle public spending cuts as the sectors of the economy that live off public expenses took to the streets and interfered with traffic, during increasingly violent protests.

With the debt about to explode, investors panicked. Just five months after the announcement of the zero deficit policy the crisis worsened. President De La Rúa had to resign on December 21, 2001, faced with an indignant population that was not allowed withdraw their money from the banks, general social unrest, falling fiscal revenues, and an unchecked deficit.

A few days later, an interim administration headed by Adolfo Rodríguez Sáa made the remarkable announcement of officially defaulting on the public debt owed to private creditors, which threatened the very existence of local banks (which held large amounts of government bonds). Although the interim administration lasted only five days in office, the default decision (applauded by the legislative assembly) was embraced by the incoming Duhalde administration.

Confiscation of Bank Deposits: The Argentine Government Commits the Perfect Crime

On December 3, 2001, Argentine citizens woke up to the news that they would be unable to withdraw their deposits from the banks, deposits which totaled 86 billion dollars in January 2001, one and a half time the national budget, and over half of the country's public debt. Deposits dropped to a historic low after months' of withdrawals that left them at under 70 billion dollars by January 2002. The government colluded with local banks which were bond holders in order to protect them from further withdrawals through a presidential legal decree. The absence of institutions with the capacity to limit the government's voracity led directly to the greatest robbery of the century.

The government's desperate measures to avoid defaulting on the debt led to the great bank robbery: bank deposits were frozen, dollar deposits were converted into worthless bonds, and private loans were denominated in pesos. This was the perfect crime. And just like the French economist Frederic Bastiat had written over a century earlier, the government by the power of its own law, robbed the population with the most absolute impunity.

Spontaneous protests by the population through noisy demonstrations known as *cacerolazos* forced President Fernando de la Rua to resign on December 21, 2001.

By Christmas, 2001, Argentina declared the largest default in history on its 132 billion dollar debt and abandoned Convertibility, causing uncontrolled devaluation of the currency and the conversion of debts denominated in dollars into pesos.

In his article *Canada sleeps as Argentina plunders*, Cato Institute scholar Steve Hanke suggests that the worst losers of all this have been foreigners, with foreign banks losing close to 12 billion dollars. But he is ignoring the magnitude of what was taken from the Argentines themselves as depositors (70 billion dollars), as holders of a significant portion of government bonds (132 billion dollars), and as future retirees forced by the AFJP regime to "invest" in domestic banks and in public bonds which the government stopped servicing.

The public responded with hundreds of marches and demonstrations and protests against the complicity between banks and the government. Banks hid behind the administration's decree to deny depositors access to what they owned, treating all depositors alike.

Although the Argentine Constitution clearly defends private property rights in sections 14 and 17, the judicial branch has yet to issue judgment on the confiscation of savings. The failure of institutions and the discredit to the justice system has driven many depositors to bring action at the main offices of foreign banks, mainly in the United States and in Spain. And a spontaneous association has formed to defend the rights of depositors, the Asociación de Ahorristas Estafados por el Estado (Association of Depositors Embezzled by the State), led by Nito Artaza, an actor and show-business entrepreneur.

Moreover, *pesofication* means that all Argentines will have to pay the losses of debtors, just as the devaluation of the peso gives an artificial advantage to domestic products over imports, an advantage that will vanish according to projected inflation figures. Power groups for *pesofication* of private dollar debts (pushed dollar) at the rate of one peso per dollar, charging the national State with the difference through default of the debt.

In late 2002, Argentina became a country fragmented into sectors that demand increasingly conflicting rights (bank customers vs. banks, manufacturers vs. farmers, creditors vs. debtors, landlords vs. tenants, workers vs. employers, teachers vs. government, Congress vs. the Supreme Court, the provinces vs. the national executive, small retailers vs. large store chains, etc.), as if everybody were aware that the pie is small and forever destined to not grow. So the rational decision seems to be to try to get as much from the pie as one can without taking into account justice, cooperation, or growth.

The default on debt payments, the devaluation, the measures known as the *corralito* (the freezing of bank deposits), and the measures that converted dollar debts into pesos amount to the violation of millions of private agreements. These agreements rested on rules that lacked basic legal protections. In the absence of basic societal rules, the State once again acted as arbiter of rewards and punishments. And with measures (like the devaluation or *pesofication* of debts) that favored influential groups, the savings of the population vanished, relations with foreign business creditors were left in disarray as were mortgage and rent agreements in the domestic market.

The Argentine financial system collapsed with the robbery of the savings of generations of Argentines to finance the fiscal excesses of the government. No one in the country trusts the banking system, since all banks held defaulted government bonds which represent 30 percent face value of the new bonds.

In 2003 Kirchner was elected President and through the collapse of imports and record exports due to high commodities prices (grains and oil) Argentina has had extraordinary balance of payment surplus. This together with import substitution the GNP grew 9 percent p.a. in 2003, 2004 and 8 percent estimated for 2005. Notwithstanding this we still have an unemployment of 20 percent and 40 percent of the population below poverty levels.

The End of Convertibility or the Awakening of the Leviathan

> *If the community does not restore credit, the State's only option will be to finance itself through the inflationary tax, or the financial system will go bankrupt because its main debtor is unable to cancel its debts* — FIEL Report, May 1989

The Argentine State reminds us of the Leviathan, the monster from Greek mythology used by political philosopher Thomas Hobbes to represent the natural voracity of the state, in reference to monarchical absolutism. The public sector appealed to a wide range of financing sources to survive intact, so that once credit sources were no longer unavailable and tax revenues started to drop, unrestricted issuing of currency became the tool of choice for politicians.

With the default and the end of convertibility of the Argentine peso, the hands of the Leviathan have been untied and the money issuing machine has been brought out of the retirement imposed by Convertibility in 1991. The end of convertibility also meant abandoning strategic priorities set by the government, such as reducing the cost of politics, reforming the inefficient State, restoring legal protections, property rights, and the agreements violated with the confiscation of bank deposits.

The abandonment of convertibility, achieved by altering of the charter of the Central Bank allowed the government to revert to financing its imbalanced accounts by issuing currency without backing, reducing the purchasing power of its citizens through the so-called inflationary tax. This new scenario requires neither fiscal equilibrium nor efficiency in the allocation of public resources, and it ignores the reforms necessary to revive the agonizing Argentine economy.

The administration of President Eduardo Duhalde came into office on January 2, 2002, bringing along a coalition of political and economic interest groups consistent with the return to an interventionist and closed economy, one that arbitrarily hands out privileges to the few and imposes costs on society at large. Pesofication of bank deposits at 1.40 pesos per dollar, when the current free market exchange rate is close to 3 pesos means that the State is trampling on the property rights of depositors and on private agreements, while the pesofication of the debts of corporations and individuals clearly benefited domestic economic groups that wield great political influence.

Devaluation was welcome by industrial sectors, which had long clamored for closing the economy. The devaluation of the peso meant that the price of imports almost tripled, and, as a result, in the first eight months of 2002 imports fell by 70 percent, putting producers—not consumers—at the helm of the domestic market again. The ideological basis for the economic policy of this government is none other than the old ECLAC model, based on income redistribution as a tool for boosting the domestic market, and closing the economy to prevent the expected increase in demand to vanish in the form of increased imports.

A State Hostage to Interest Groups

Sadly, Argentina is the perfect example of a State taken over by highly organized interest groups which exploit the rest of society. Will Argentina ever break this vicious rent-seeking cycle and focus on generating wealth?

Mancur Olson, the late economist from the University of Maryland, wrote that economic growth becomes impossible when "distribution coalitions," or interest groups, take the reins of a country. These interest coalitions are comparable to what James Buchanan calls rent-seeking groups, which attempt to obtain privileges or special treatment that diminish or hinder the creation of social wealth. In Argentina, the inflexibility of reducing public spending and the persistence of closed and highly regulated markets is due to the fact that the least economically productive sectors have been most efficient in preserving rules that favor them. Among these sectors are the "political class," those that depend on public spending, inefficient manufacturers, and unions, all of whom make serious institutional change, impossible.

The events of 2000 and 2001 show that all that was solid evaporated into thin air, and the progress made with the "reforms" of the 1990s disappeared like water between the fingers. The chart below shows that those institutions intended to limit the actions of government were crushed one by one, allowing a return to the previous state of affairs. Thus, convertibility of the peso evaporated with the politicization of the Central Bank, which was supposed to uphold the value of the peso. And as the bimonetary financial system collapsed, the government passed a statute (Ley de Intangibilidad de los Depósitos or Law of Intangibility of Deposits)[189] which turned out to be the preamble to the imminent embezzlement of depositors. The same fate was shared by holders of bonds issued by the Argentine government.

Chronology of Institutional Collapse

Date	Institutional Failure	Institution Affected	President
April 2001	End of the autonomy of the Central Bank (Ministers Cavallo-Pou)	Independence of Central Bank	Fernando De la Rúa
May 2001	"Expansion" of Convertibility through the inclusion of the Euro at a rate of 1 to 1 with the US dollar	Monetary regime	Fernando De la Rúa
October 2001	Intangibility of deposits	False certainty about the currency of origin of bank deposits	Fernando De la Rúa
December 2001	Initial financial restrictions on bank withdrawals (*corralito*)	Restrictions on free disposition of bank deposits (originally for 90 days)	Fernando De la Rúa
January 2002	Non payment of debt to private creditors Default foreign debt	Rights of creditors— local and foreign	Adolfo Rodríguez Saá
	End of Convertibility and devaluation of the peso	Violation of the rights of holders of pesos. Altering the terms of domestic and foreign agreements	Eduardo Duhalde
	Asymmetrical pesofication	Commercial banks	Duhalde

Date	Institutional Failure	Institution Affected	President
February 2002	Further restrictions on term deposits and prohibition to close unpaid mortgages	Property rights	Duhalde
May 2003	Price control on public service tariffs	Contracts between government and private enterprises	Kirchner
March 2004	Retention of exports of agricultural and oil products	Asymmetrical taxes to export groups	Kirchner
April 2005	Agreement default	Creditor/debtor	Kirchner

Throughout its history, Argentina has been unable to limit the voracity of a State that remained accessible to powerful interest groups even at a time of supposed openness like the 1990s. Mario Teijeiro defines the spirit of what he calls "corporative" rather than competitive capitalism, as applied by the Argentine administration during the 1990s:

> When it comes to doing business, we want a partner–State to protect our markets, define the strategic profile, choose winners by sanctioning monopolies, industrial promotion, special tax regimes, subsidies to certain sectors or regions, and other privileges. But, since protecting all sectors simultaneously is by definition impossible (the "business" of protection is at best a zero sum game), the partner State always ends up choosing winners and losers. Later on, when the economic crisis comes, it is time for revenge. Policies previously used to choose winners become an instrument to compensate losers and punish winners. However, in order to do this, first, the stability of the rules of the game must be destroyed. Along the way, we lose basic capitalist institutions and destroy the most basic trust of depositors and investors. Corporative capitalism holds the seeds for self-destruction. To expect corporative capitalism to work in Argentina is like expecting a good outcome from a soccer game played between rival gangs, without rules and without a referee ... Impossible.

Power Groups Block Reform

Recent history would appear to indicate that any institutional change is impossible in Argentina. Those who would lose from a substantial change in the rules of the game have been politically stronger and have won the battle, aborting any and all chance of change. Decades of closed economies and political systems have fed these parasitic groups that live off the rest of society and benefit from the current state of affairs; they are highly organized and efficient in influencing public policy decisions.

Mancur Olson wrote in his *The Rise and Decline of Great Nations*[190] that successful nations like Italy and Germany slowly decelerated their growth until reaching virtual paralysis as a consequence of the accumulation of special interest groups. In those instances, a lateral effect of the defeat in World War II was the possibility of starting anew institutionally and reshuffling the previous concentration of power in those societies. The name Olson gives these groups, "distributional coalitions," is equivalent to James Buchanan's "rent-seeking groups."

In such an environment, uncontrolled growth in public spending in the 1990s, the persistence of white elephants, that is, sectors that remained impervious to change, the devaluation demanded by inefficient industrial sectors and the return of a monetary regime based on spurious currency emission, are clear indicators of the triumph of the coalition opposed to change.

A salient feature of these white elephants is the fascist-inspired labor regime, which did not undergo radical modification during the 1990s, leaving unchanged the legislation that imposes high costs to the hiring of workers and preserves union power. This added costs are mostly in terms of direct and indirect mandatory contributions that go in large part to finance unions. Similarly, restrictions that consolidated the rigidity of the labor market remain, such as high severance payments, the payment of a 13th month in wages, "or annual complementary salary," vacation time, etc. This regime, intended to help workers, is a huge obstacle to hiring workers, with the employer contributing between 50 percent and 100 percent over the wages paid to the worker. All of this explains an unemployment rate that grew from eight percent in 1995 to 22 percent in 2002.

The Union Health Systems are at the center of the economic and political power that unions wield, and it allows exploiting captive members who are resigned to a system with no prospect of improvement. This monopolistic and mandatory system of delivery of health services is facing inevitable collapse. A large portion of the Union Health Systems are practically bankrupt, and face serious difficulties in providing basic services such as hospital services or the purchase of medicinal drugs, which has left their members totally unprotected. A report by Gustavo Mammoni, President of the Federation of Clinics and Hospitals of the province of Buenos Aires (FECLIBA) states that Union Health Systems owe over two billion pesos to health care providers, which means that services are routinely denied.[191] The same report states that almost 50 percent of the population lacks any health coverage. The failure of the Union Health Systems are also evident in the fact that a substantial portion of the population subscribes to private health care insurance in addition to the low quality health care they are forced to pay.

The crisis in the role of the state in the field of health is evident not only in the failure of Union Health Systems but also in public hospitals whose purpose is to provide care to the portion of the population which is in need. The absence of market incentives has turned public hospitals into entrenched bureaucracies with minimal accountability toward an impoverished captive, and desperate public, which in many cases is unaware of its rights as citizens. This situation is made even more untenable inasmuch as after four years of recession, more and more people have lost private coverage and even coverage from the Union Health Systems, and thus add pressure on a system that is incapable of covering their needs.

The country's closed public education system remains unchanged. So much so, that Ricardo López Murphy, Finance Minister under Presidente de la Rúa, was forced to resign just days after being named to the post, after proposing slight reductions in the budgets of state universities. Public education is an instrument of control, which is exerted through one-size-fits-all educational programs and intended to satisfy a niche of political clients that make it very socially expensive. They are overextended and overpopulated, because they are free of charge, access is unrestricted, and there is no control over the academic performance of students. Some students take as long as 10, 20 or 30 years to complete their education, which has a negative impact on the costs of public education. There is a surprisingly low correlation between graduates and students per year (3.4 percent), and the cost per graduate ($45,000) is equivalent to the budgeted cost of 30 students ($1,500), which tells us how many do manage to graduate.

In the face of the resounding failure of the Argentine State in providing services such as health — both in the case of the Union Health System as in public hospitals— education, unemployment ,and aid to the poor, it is clear that the way to offer an effective way to help those in need is through quasi-market institutions that publicly finance services provided by the private sector in a competitive framework, as is the case with *vouchers* or bonds aimed at guaranteeing competitive quality at a reasonable and controlled social cost. These schemes would directly affect the interests of traditional power groups.

Conclusion

Can substantial changes in the basic rules happen in Argentina? Spain emerged from decades of fiscal imbalances and political authoritarianism, and its fiscal policy is now tied to the policies of the Bundesbank. In Latin

America, while many countries travel the same erratic road as Argentina. Two countries, Chile and Mexico, became members of NAFTA which meant positive growth rates and the end of the political monopoly of the PRI — are breaking the chains of poverty-inducing institutions. This gives us hope that trade will be the answer by corroding the power bases of traditional groups and planting the seeds of change.

9
Toward a Competitive Federalism

The Federalism That Never Happened

As was noted earlier, Latin American countries in general, and Argentina in particular, have failed to place constraints on their governments' interventionism in the allocation of resources and their interference in voluntary exchanges. High concentrations of power have given rise to societies where the State has unlimited ability to reassign resources, taking from one group and giving to another, and perpetuating rules that encourage anti competitive behavior.

Juan Bautista Alberdi, the author of the Argentine Constitution of 1853, took inspiration from the different constitutions of the United States when looking for the formula to break the burdensome tradition of concentration of power by government. In the republican division of powers and in federalism he found the basis for forging a strategy. Alberdi warned of the uphill battle that the new rules would face in attempting to revert the local tradition of centralism and saw immigration as an instrument to change Hispanic customs and traditions.

Centralism as an Indelible Legacy

At the time of independence in Latin America, there was no precedent for either federalism or limits to central power; the region's legacy was the firm centralism implemented by the Crown. "Federal" regimes adopted by most of the newly independent Latin American countries built on centralist institutional traditions, which prevailed over newly sanctioned laws. This is clearly evident in taxation, education, health, and social security.

Imperial Spanish centralism has remained indelibly in the organization of Latin American countries. In economic terms, centralism constitutes a 'political failure' that misallocates economic resources, generating noise between the demand of consumer-voters and the producer-politicians. In *Hacia una nueva organización del federalismo fiscal*, by FIEL (Fundación de Investigaciones Económicas Latinoamericanas), we see how decentralization of responsibilities brings public decision making as close as possible to taxpayers and voters. More decentralized forms of government lead to genuine democratization and to a higher degree of citizen involvement in politics. This position is consistent with the principles of competition, efficiency, and decentralization of economic, union, and political power.[192]

Incentives for orderly and socially convenient behavior are also lost under the current system. Maximizing spending and then receiving subsidies and bailouts from the national government have been a long held practice. The pressure to spend more has held sway, since the bulk of the responsibility for financing additional outlays is passed on to other jurisdictions. This dissociation between the decision to spend and the obligation to pay it back generates, inevitably, great global inefficiencies.[193]

According to FIEL, decentralization offers two basic economic advantages. The first in *fiscal correspondence*. The criterion of fiscal correspondence is satisfied when those who benefit directly from public spending have to support its financing. In the centralized model, the close link between the decision to increase public spending and the consequent tax increases has been broken, and voters have less incentive to oppose inefficient raises in state outlays. This is precisely why in most countries there is a close correlation between tax powers and spending responsibilities, even when it could be shown that greater centralization in revenue collection would be more efficient.

Decentralization has the additional advantage of clearly establishing the relative price of tax-public expenditures, that is, that the marginal tax burden on taxpayers is tied to adequate service provision. Given the global restriction on resources, higher public spending means less private spending, or more clearly, it means a lower remuneration for the factors of production, especially labor and land, which are less mobile.

The following quote by Adam Smith shows that the recommendation to keep the taxpayer close to spending decisions has been with us for many centuries:

> Even those public works which are of such a nature that they cannot afford any revenue for maintaining themselves, but of which the

convenience is nearly confined to some particular place or district, are always better maintained by a local or provincial revenue, under the management of a local or provincial administration, than by the general revenue of the state, of which the executive power must always have the management. Were the streets of London to be lighted and paved at the expense of the treasury, is there any probability that they would be so well lighted and paved as they are at present, or even at so small an expense? The expense, besides, instead of being raised by a local tax upon the inhabitants of each particular street, parish or district in London, would, in this case, be defrayed out of the general revenue of the state, and would consequently be raised by a tax upon all the inhabitants of the kingdom, of whom the greater part derive no sort of benefit from the lighting and paving of the streets of London.

The abuses which sometimes creep into the local and provincial administration of a local and provincial revenue, how enormous soever they may appear, are in reality, however, almost always, very trifling in comparison of those which commonly take place in the administration and expenditure of the revenue of a great empire. They are, besides, much more easily corrected.[194]

The other basic advantage of decentralization is *political responsibility*. This criterion is satisfied when politicians are accountable to voters for the quality of public policies. Accountability and control are greater the closer the voter is to the political level that decides and implements public policies. A related issue, although not economic in nature, is that bringing decisions closer to the level of the individual citizen means decentralizing power and increasing participation and control by civil society.

James Buchanan, who developed the theory of competitive federalism, writes that the normative theory of competitive federalism is congenial to economists, in particular, because it extends the principles of the market economy to the organization of the political structure.[195] The market economy produces high levels of value that benefit all participants; individuals have legally protected rights to enter and exit production and exchange relations. If a product or service is offered by a producer-seller but the terms are unacceptable, the potential consumer-buyer simply exercises the exit option and looks for an alternate provider. Thus, federalism offers a means of introducing the main aspects of the market into politics. Federalism serves two purposes: reduces the scope of the central government and, at the same time, limits the potential for exporting citizens by the state-province units.

In summary, centralism appears to be one of the most ingrained institutions in the history of Latin America, and has survived in spite of the largely federal constitutions sanctioned after independence and of economic reform processes implemented in the last two decades. Key to the survival of centralism has been the management of national revenue by the central government.

TABLE 9-1
The Legacy of the Centralist Tradition Today
(Constrast with the United States)

	Latin America	United States
Fiscal Correspondence	No	Yes
Political responsibility	Diffuse	Direct
Election system	Multi candidate list	Single candidate by district
	Voting is Mandatory	Voting is voluntary
Party discipline	Competition between political parties	Monopolistic or with high barriers to individuals running for office
Management of public goods	Centralized, national or provincial	Decentralized at local level
Public safety	National and provincial police chief	Sheriff, elected by citizens vote
Role of towns and counties	Minor, the last rung in the chain of delegation	Essential role, the first rung in the priority of delegation

The Argentine Case

The predominance of informal traditions and customs over the functioning of society is quite clear in the case of the balance between federalism and centralism in Argentina. Although the Constitution of 1853 clearly established a federal system as a tool to protect citizens against arbitrary action by the State, the actual organization of the country was manifestly centralist, with a unitary fiscal regime and tradition.

In contrast, in the United States, federalism came naturally and as a consequence of the institutional evolution of old traditions. Its implementation, then, did not involve applying some theory foreign to local practices, but was more the natural result of the union of independent colonies, which established their own rules and determined their levels of taxation. Thus, the federal government was given specific and limited functions—which eventually expanded—that allowed it to collect certain taxes, with localities maintaining the right to collect their own.

In Argentina, the tax organization has been moving toward centralization, with the nation gaining on the provinces. The history of the fiscal relations between nation and provinces can be divided into three phases. The first goes from 1853 to 1890. During this phase, there existed a system of clear separation of tax revenue. The national State paid for its expenditure out of revenue from foreign trade and domestic taxes on then national territories—Chaco, La Pampa, Misiones, Formosa, Neuquen, Santa Cruz, Río Negro and Chubut—which became provinces in the 1950s. On the other hand, provinces financed their expenditures with taxes on property and consumption. Consolidated public spending was under 10 percent of GDP, and provincial spending amounted to less than 30 percent of that figure. There was fiscal discipline; provincial governments were autonomous, with less than 5 percent of expenditures depending on transfers from the national government. And since each level of government had its clearly defined sphere of competence, there was no need for coordination between the national state and the provinces.

The fiscal crisis brought about by the Baring panic in 1890 proved the vulnerability of the nation's foreign tax base and animated the first debate on tax federalism since the sanction of the constitution. The issue was whether there was a constitutional constraint that prevented the nation from permanently collecting domestic taxes throughout the country. The winning position was that of the Finance Minister, Vicente F. López, who argued that the constitution contained no such objections.

The provinces agreed to confer that right on the nation, with the proviso that it be renewed yearly. This permanently altered the nation-provinces relationship. National transfers went from financing 6.5 percent of provincial expenditure in 1900 to 11.5 percent in 1910. Through ad hoc channels of repayment and redistribution, the nation returned the right the provinces had conferred. The relationship between per capita public spending in the more advanced provinces and per capita public spending in the less developed ones began to favor the latter, until the early 1930s.[196]

During the second phase, from 1890 to 1935, a de facto system of concurrence prevailed. The salient feature of this phase was a tax on consumption implemented by the nation, which overlapped with one already collected by the provinces, to make up for the unstable and unpredictable revenues from foreign trade.

Senator Jorge Capitanich writes that the National Constitution of 1853 established in Sections 4 and Section 67, subsection 27, a strict system of separation of revenue sources. However, later interpretations granted the nation the power to collect resources from indirect taxes concurrently with the provinces, establishing expressly that the latter reserved the right to collect direct taxes. Nevertheless, this was bypassed in 1935, when income taxes were established and a systematic legal mechanism forced the provinces to cede resources to the nation.

The third phase covers 1935 to the present and is marked by the consolidation of the system of allocation or coparticipation of taxes which awards the nation the main role for levying direct taxes.[197] Coparticipation was sanctioned in 1935 through Acts 12.139, 12.143 y 12.147, which massively augmented the resources available to the nation. New sales and income taxes were created, and existing domestic taxes were codified and unified. In later decades, the scheme was modified to enlarge the pool of funds for coparticipation. Finally, Act 23.548, in effect since January 1988 with its various amendments, established a temporary arrangement for distribution of tax revenues between the nation and the provinces.

According to this temporary regime, the total amount of national taxes collected — with the exception of foreign trade duties and taxes collected for specific purposes— had to be distributed according to the provisions of section 3 of Act 23.548:

- 42.34% for the nation
- 54.66% to all the provinces
- 2% as compensation for the provinces of Buenos Aires (1.5701%), Chubut (0.1433%), Neuquen (0.1433%), and Santa Cruz (0.1433%).
- 1% for the National Treasury Fund for the Provinces.

In 1973, the system was materially changed with the creation of the VAT. The primary distribution was established at 48.5 percent for the nation and a similar percentage to be distributed among the provinces, with the remainder going to a compensating pool. The second big change was that the system became redistributive. That is, the secondary distribution (the formula for allocating revenue among the provinces) no longer depended on the contribution that each province made to the total collection, but rather, it gave way to a redistributive system, where the most productive provinces began to subsidize the less productive ones.

TABLE 9-2
Federal Coparticipation Regime
(1935–1998)

Act	Period	Nation	Provinces and City of Buenos Aires
12.143 and 12.147	1935–1946	82.5	17.5
12.956	1947–1958	79.0	21.0
14.788	1959	66.0	34.0
	1960	64.0	36.0
	1961	62.0	38.0
	1962	60.0	40.0
	1963	58.0	42.0
	1964–1966	54.0	46.0
	1967	59.2	40.8
	1968–1972	61.9	38.1
20.221	1973–1980	46.7	53.3
23.548	1981–1984	48.5	51.5
	1988	42.34	57.66
Fiscal Pacts and Amendments to Act 23.548	1991–1992–1993	49.36	50.64

Source: Cetrángolo and Jiménez, *Algunas reflexiones sobre el federalismo fiscal en la Argentina*, Centro de Estudios para el Cambio Estructural, Buenos Aires, 1996.

Federal Revenue Coparticipation: An Invitation to Spend More

The federal revenue coparticipation regime is one of the pillars of the chronic fiscal irresponsibility that has brought Argentina to its terminal crisis. From an economic perspective, coparticipation is a redistributive system that completely divorces a province's tax collection from its revenue stream, creating cross-subsidies that encourage greater bureaucratic spending and moves decisions away from taxpayer control. Governors and mayors enjoy the benefit of spending but do not pay the cost of raising taxes.

According to Jorge Ávila (economist of CEMA, Buenos Aires), the coparticipation regime has three main consequences: it magnifies the public provincial spending, it reduces compliance with tax laws, and rewards provincial lobbying efforts to obtain a larger portion of the federal funds. Coparticipation is a common pool and at present accounts for the fact that over 60 percent of provincial public spending is funded through national funds, a fact that would be better described as a unitary, rather than a federal system. In some extreme cases, such as the provinces of Catamarca, La Rioja, and Formosa, 93 percent of provincial spending is financed with national funds. The author gives the following example to illustrate the logic of the regime:

> I live in Buenos Aires but am originally from San Juan. During one visit back home at my mother's house, I noticed improvements being done to a nearby park. I asked her opinion of the work, and, to my surprise, she did not seem to be aware of the construction. I asked her if she was being charged extra taxes but she answered no. Again, I asked if she would have preferred that the monies be used for building a new wing to the Rawson Hospital or new classrooms for the Sarmiento school. Now tired of my questions, she exclaimed: "Let them improve the park. It's money from Buenos Aires anyway!" We know it is not money from Buenos Aires, since both coparticipation and other federal monies come from revenue collected throughout the country. Yet, my mother's reasoning is impeccable. She pays her taxes but sees no connection between her tax effort and additional spending decisions in her province. And she sees no connection because there is none. The national government incurs the political cost of collecting, the province gets the benefit of spending the resources, and the taxpayer is an indifferent witness to funds coming and going. There is no incentive to control, get angry, and demand that local public monies be well spent.[198]

As economist Roberto Cachanosky writes, the country's present system is federal in its spending and unitary in its collection. Thus, governors and mayors enjoy the benefit of spending without facing the political cost of collecting taxes. Of the almost $100 billion pesos of the country's aggregate annual public spending (including all jurisdictions), $49.5 billion are spent by the nation, $38 billion by the provinces, and $12.5 billion by municipalities. These figures show that the nation controls only 50 percent of the consolidated public expenditures, and also explain why international financial agencies, in particular, attribute such high importance to the negotiations which are once again under way between the national government and governors to settle fiscal figures. In the year 2000, 66 percent of aggregate spending by all provinces and the government of the city of Buenos Aires went to "social public spending." Between 1992 and 2000, this type of spending by the provinces grew by $8.377 billion. The other item that grew significantly in the provinces was servicing the public debt. For the same period, interest on the provincial public debt grew 82 percent, from $5.580 billion to $10.141 billion. Spending on interest, a consequence of fiscal deficit, has reached 20 percent of total spending up from 13 percent in 1992. Indebtedness was another mechanism used heavily by the provinces to finance their expenses. In September of last year, the public debt stock of Buenos Aires amounted to $7.275 billion, or 127.7 percent of the province's total tax revenues and coparticipation funds for a whole year. The debt of the province of Rio Negro was 268 percent of its annual revenues, while the figure for Chaco was 238.6 percent.[199]

The excess in public spending that this regime brings about is clear when we look at the increase in spending by level of government. Between 1992 and 2000, federal spending grew by 35 percent, provinces by 57 percent and municipal spending by 48 percent. However, the quality of the spending does not seem to have kept pace with its actual growth.

Competitive Federalism

The evidence we have presented so far shows that, regardless of the country's formal federalism, Argentina and Latin America are clearly centralist countries with both a tradition and a fiscal regime that are unitary. The consequence of the coparticipation scheme which is different in each country is encouraging more rather than less public spending.

The United States, on the contrary, became a federal union of independent colonies that passed their own laws and determined their tax burdens. At the time of the union, they assigned the federal government precise and limited functions, ceding to it the revenue from certain levies but retaining the right to collect them. This is the system that currently governs that country's public finances and the same system that keeps public spending within reasonable levels thanks to taxpayer control at the state and county levels.

Unless a radical change is effected in the rules of the game, it is unthinkable that there will ever be rationality in Argentina's public finances. The implementation of a scheme consistent with "competitive federalism" would help bring down the level of public spending, through greater control by citizens and taxpayers.

What do we mean by "competitive federalism?" The system rests on the application of two basic principles: first, each province must set its own level of taxation; second, each province collects taxes for its own jurisdiction and those federal taxes that will be subsequently be transferred to the national government. Thus, the pyramid is inverted and taxpayers regain control over their government.

James Buchanan, who founded the public choice school of economics, stresses the role of federalism in limiting government interference. In "Federalism and Individual Sovereignty," he writes that federalism offers the means for introducing the main elements of the market into politics. Moreover, by enabling a division of power, it tends to limit coercion. He goes on to develop the theory of "competitive federalism" as an extension of the tenets of the market economy to the organization of the political structure. For Buchanan, the incentives generated by competition among jurisdictions, together with the direct control by taxpayers over the level of spending and services are the only way to guarantee quality and cost effective state services.[200]

In the United States, the federal government collects income taxes. Each state may establish rates and collect income and/or sales tax. Local government units collect property taxes which pay for some or all of the costs of education, public safety, etc. The federal government is financed mainly through income and social security taxes. Each level of government finances more than 80 percent of its spending with only two sources of tax revenue (the federal government 81 percent, the states 83 percent, and local governments 88 percent), as the following chart shows.

TABLE 9-3
Financing of the Different Levels of Government in the United States
(% of Total Collections)

Type of Tax	Federal	State	Local
Total	100	100	100
Property	0	2	72
Sales	3	48	16
Personal income	48	35	5
Corporate Income	11	6	1
Excise on automobiles	0	3	0
Social Security	33	0	0
Other	4	6	5

Source: Author, with IRS figures.

It is clear that the coparticipation scheme needs to be scratched for the country's public finances to once again respond to the needs of taxpayers, restoring the federal principles established in the National Constitution and returning autonomy to each of the provinces.

This proposal calls for each jurisdiction to establish its own revenues and expenditures, while the national government does the same with its own, collecting revenue and fixing its level of spending. The adoption of competitive federalism in Latin America would have the following implications:

Provincial Bureaucracies Will Adjust to Their Genuine Revenues

Each province shall subsist with no more than the revenues collected from its own economy, eliminating cross subsidies that at present serve to swell bureaucracies and provincial spending. With the application of this system, Latin America should undergo a major change, with deficit-ridden provinces adjusting to their real revenues. The same should be true of the national government.

Competition for Investment

Well-managed provinces with orderly finances will be able to reduce their tax rates and attract investments, both of which will result in benefits for its residents. In contrast, those with high taxes and more burdensome bureaucracies will suffer not only the lack of investment but also the vote of its residents. Thus, an efficient government will be a competitive advantage, rather than an ever heavier burden on the private sector.

Taxpayer Control Over the Level and Transparency of Provincial Public Spending

Since decisions are made at the micro rather than the macro level, incentives are toward better goods and services provided at a lower cost. In this sense, it is worth noting Oates's theorem, which states that a decentralized service provision will always be more efficient because local governments are better informed about the preferences of the electorate. Thus, resource allocation will more closely match the preferences of consumers.[201]

Provincial Control Over the Nation's Spending

The pyramid would be turned upside down, and it would fall on the provinces to ensure that the nation's public spending is efficient, precluding the quasi extortive situations to which they are presently subjected.

Given this diagnosis, our proposal is for the adoption of "competitive federalism" in Latin America that is to transfer to the provincial level of the establishment of tax rates and the collection for the following levies now being collected by the federal governments: Value Added Tax, excise taxes, personal property, fuel and other levies. The federal government, on the other hand, will temporarily keep revenue from income tax, projected income tax following year, tax on credit-debit operations in checking accounts, foreign trade and Social Security taxes to be applied to the functions not delegated to the provinces (Justice, Defense, Foreign Relations), as well as the repayment of the public debt and the obligation to the present beneficiaries of the social security system. Once the transition is complete, that is, when the public debt and the debt to the social security systems have been paid off, only the Corporate Income Tax (at present, corporate and individual income taxes) and taxes levied on foreign trade will remain in the hands of the national government.

TABLE 9-4
Tax Appropriation Under the New Scheme

Tax	Revenue	%	Nation	Provinces
Income	10.0	22	10	
VAT	15.3	34		15.3
ExciseInternos	1.6	4		1.6
Ganancia Presunta	0.5	1	0.5	
Personal Property	0.7	2		0.7
Credit-debit operations in checking accounts	2.9	6	2.9	
Foreign trade	1.6	4	1.6	
Fuel	3.2	7		3.2
Social Security	8.0	18	8.0	
Other	1.6	4		1.6
TOTAL	45.4	100	23	22.4

In the following chapter we will address in depth the supply of education, health, security, social security, and other services in the context of municipal and provincial administrations.

The following institutional requirements must be satisfied to maximize the benefits of competitive federalism:

- establishing institutional ceilings for tax increases. This should comprise: a) a maximum limit in the rates of each type of levy; b) a maximum consolidated tax; c) a ruling from the Supreme Court of Justice regarding the maximum tax that can be charged to taxpayers.
- reduction in the costs of entering and exiting both for persons and corporations in each province.

- labor, administrative and tax deregulation.
- reduction in the costs of the administration of the tax system (both the budget of the pension plans should reduce the costs of compliance on persons and corporations).

It should be noted that a proposal for competitive federalism does not solve the problems of the deficit and high spending levels. It simply gives governments the necessary incentives for better allocating public resources. Consequently, lower spending levels and a proper allocation of resources will derive from the implementation of competitive federalism.

The implementation of competitive federalism is the first necessary step to ensure adequate fiscal correspondence, a rational level of public spending, and the appropriate provision of public goods.

10
Vested Interests Block Institutional Change

When we wonder why institutional change is so hard to achieve in Latin American societies given the repeated and evident failures of attempts at reform, we should point out that the interests defending the status quo are extremely powerful.

Even though society at large is hurt by the steady decline in living conditions, there are clear winners in the scheme of redistribution and destruction of wealth, whose interests would be seriously affected by a change toward more open rules and institutions.

Such is the case with political and union groups that benefit from managing public sector resources with the goal of consolidating their own power through clientelism (the exchange between politicians and voters of material private goods for votes), as well as businessmen who strive to obtain special privileges–be they monopolies, public contracts, import duties, or debt reduction — and can obtain extraordinary income through nonmarket factors. Thus, a sector of the population with concentrated interests and the ability to determine public policies perpetuates rules of the game that allow one sector of society to exploit the other. The less efficient producers are most efficient at influencing the public decision making process.

Argentina's big bang of 2001–2002 is a clear instance of the triumph of the redistributive groups in the struggle to dismantle restrictions to monetary emission and of the relative economic openness enabled by the convertibility law and its nominal exchange rate of one peso per dollar. The end of this regime — with its concomitant devaluation of the peso, the default on the debt incurred with private creditors, confiscation and "pesofication" of bank deposits— meant clear benefits for specific public and private interest groups which were highly leveraged and were able to reduce their debt by a third in one stroke.

For the finances of the federal government, it meant unilaterally postponing the payment of debt commitments with private creditors, the return to monetary emission as a means of financing the public sector, and the establishment of export duties to subsidize social spending and reinforce clientelism.

The devaluation of the peso—from a one to one correspondence with the US dollar between March 1991 and December of 2001 to three pesos per dollar by mid–2002—for the entrenched industrial interests, born and bred under a regime of import substitution, meant expelling international competitors from the domestic market. The year after the big devaluation, imports fell by half in Argentina.

This recent example points to a system of interests that reinforces rent-seeking rules and institutions in the region and benefits from the continued existence of redistributive systems. In recent decades, these interests have acquired a life of their own, like a monster demanding more public resources and a greater intervention of the state in the private sphere. Their growing voracity constantly demands more resources, which are obtained through both traditional means—higher taxes and public indebtedness—and other more creative subterfuges such as confiscation of time and current bank deposits and default on the debt.

Another mainstay of financing for the voracious Latin American governments is oil revenues, which in the region tend to go to the state. Venezuela and Mexico are the more obvious instances of this. In "Oil Revenue Assignment: Country Experiences and Issues," Ehtisham Ahmad and Eric Mottu write that oil represents an important portion of public sector revenues for some Latin American countries, such as Venezuela—where such income accounted for 47 percent of aggregate public sector revenues between 1997 and 2000—and Mexico, with a figure of 30 percent for the same period[202] while in 2004 year to date it is estimated 62 percent for Venezuela and 41 percent for Mexico.

In general terms, we can say that there is a strong correlation between the absence of constraints to financing in the public sector and the improbability of institutional change.

Clientelism as an Obstacle to Change

Latin America has an established tradition of political clientelism, in which employment in the public sector plays a key role. According to *Miami Herald* columnist Andrés Oppenheimer, scholars agree that poverty, corruption, and delinquency are the main threats to democracy in Latin

America. He should consider adding a fourth element to his list: the resurrection of social programs politically aimed at manipulating the "captive vote" in the region.

The concept of "captive vote" as a tool to reinforce political clientelism has been studied in depth at the Fundación Atlas, Buenos Aires, Argentina, with the goal of quantifying the relevance of groups of voters whose income depends on the public sector (including provincial and municipal employees, and those receiving aid from social programs). In the case of Argentina, the captive vote — including all three levels of government — constitutes about 20 percent of total voters.[203]

A recent unemployment benefits program has already had a substantial effect in this respect. Implemented in April of 2002, the Head of Household unemployment program (Plan Jefes y Jefas de Hogar) already accounts for 9.50 percent of the aggregate captive vote, that is, almost 1 out of every 2 captive voters benefits from it, and at present it covers more than 1.7 million people. The Atlas study does not include other existing social programs, such as the food program, and other provincial and municipal plans.

The Head of Household Program doubled the percentage of individuals who can be counted as captive voters. Clearly, social policy has a relevant impact on electoral results.

TABLE 10-1
Captive Vote in Argentina

National public employees	450,005
Provincial public employees	1,360,621
Municipal public employees	334,400
Total public employees	2,145,026
Beneficiaries of Head of Household unemployment program	1,772,243
Total including beneficiaries of Head of Household unemployment program	3,917,269
Total effective voters	19,930,111
Captive Vote (%)	19.60%

Oppenheimer argues that social programs perpetuate, rather than help reduce, poverty. Instead of allocating the funds to job training or to help individuals work according to their possibilities, these programs create a culture of dependency on state subsidies. In many cases, they also raise public spending and the state debt.[204]

Beyond direct public employment, there is a range of more subtle instruments, such as aid programs aimed at clientelism. This is especially the case of Venezuela under Hugo Chávez and his "missions," which are social programs that offer benefits from "grants," which are half of a minimum wage, to food baskets, priority in the distribution of land plots, and public credit, among others.

According to Venezuela's official figures, the Robinson (alphabetization), Ribas (high school education), and Sucre (post-secondary education) missions cover over 1 million individuals; Misión Vuelvan Caras, aims to create 1.2 million jobs in the farming sector; and the Plan de Salud Barrio Adentro, a health program developed with Cuban doctors for the poorer areas of the country, covers over 2 million people.

TABLE 10-2
Captive Vote in Latin America
(Excluding Aid Programs)

Country	Positive Voters (1)	Public Employees (2)	Captive Vote
Mexico	36,813,461	4,422,206	12.01%
Argentina	19,930,111	2,145,026	10.7%
Brazil	83,713,733	5,708,637	6.81%
Venezuela	6,288,578	373,482	5.93%

(1) Most recent presidential election. Source: Political database of the Americas, Georgetown University.
(2) For the three levels of government. Source: Consolidated from official statistical data of the 1990s.

If we look at the four economies with the largest GDPs in the region, captive vote (excluding aid programs) in Mexico is 12 percent, 10.7 percent in Argentina, 6.8 percent in Brazil, and 5.9 percent in Venezuela. These figures confirm the electoral significance of the manipulation of public employment. If we include aid programs for the region the percentage runs over 22 percent.

The Relevance of Import Substitution

The creation of the great urban centers surrounding the big cities of Latin America is the corollary to the import substitution processes implemented through high protectionist barriers, which strengthen power groups that favor a closed economy. Thus, Mexico's Federal district has a population of 25 million, Greater São Paulo 22 million, Greater Buenos Aires and Greater Rio de Janeiro over 12 million each; and Greater Lima more than 8 million.

These urban mega conglomerates are home to a substantial portion of the total population of each country, in the case of Greater Buenos Aires, 35 percent of Argentina's total population lives there, in Greater Lima 31 percent of Peru's and in Mexico DF 26 percent.

TABLE 10-3
Population Concentrations in the Mega Cities of Latin America

City	Population (in millions)				Mean Annual Growth Index 1980–90	Country Total Pop. 2000	Percentage of Country Total Pop. 1990
	1950	1980	1990	2000			
Buenos Aires, Argentina	5.0	9.9	11.5	12.9	1.5%	37	35%
Lima, Peru	1.0	4.4	6.2	8.2	3.4%	26	31%
Mexico D.F., Mexico	3.1	14.5	20.2	25.6	3.3%	98	26%
Rio de Janeiro, Brazil	2.9	8.8	10.7	12.5	2.0%	174	7%
São Paulo, Brazil	2.4	12.1	17.4	22.1	3.6%	174	13%

Source: Author's chart based on data from "Las ciudades latinoamericanas y el proceso de globalización," by Margarita Pérez Negrete, in Memoria: Revista mensual de política y cultura, Number 184, June 2004, Mexico D.F., and "Demographic Bulletin," Latin America and the Caribbean (1950–2050), Economic Commission for Latin America and the Caribbean, January 2004.

It is also worth noting that of the world's highest 15 urban population centers, four are located in Latin America (São Paulo, Mexico City, Buenos Aires, and Rio de Janeiro). In 1970, Latin American urban population represented 57 percent of the total region and by 1995, it had reached 73 percent with projections reaching 85 percent by 2025.[205]

Such population concentrations were encouraged by "relative prices" derived from the rules that substituted imports for national manufactures. The costs of such policies were not obvious while the world was kept at bay by high tariffs and transaction costs. However, in recent decades, average tariffs in the rest of the world have been lowered and transaction costs have fallen due to technological breakthroughs. Now, these urban centers have become unviable.

Economic policies alter market prices. These new prices act as incentives, guiding decisions to invest or disinvest, to purchase or not to purchase, and decisions to move or emigrate both by persons and corporations.

The shape of cities is influenced by incentives that are offered at the policy level. In addition to the natural incentives of spontaneous evolution, political rewards as well as overt and covert subsidies shape the morphology of whole cities and regions. Large areas have emerged and then succumbed to public policies. When public policies become unviable or are discontinued or no longer funded, countries are left with substantial problems to address. In turn, high population density has the potential to decide electoral results through the political manipulation of these votes. The vicious circle becomes impossible to break.

The strength of whole sectors of the economy that thrive under the protection of import substitution comes from the differential public policies that govern them. Automotive, chemical, textile, and capital goods industries receive preferential treatment in the context of the imperfect union that is MERCOSUR or the Comunidad Andina (formerly Andean Pact). This agreement itself has become a fortress with high tariffs for third country goods.

A study by Fundación Atlas has shown that the adoption of a common tariff in effect as of January 1, 1995 by MERCOSUR members (Argentina, Brazil, Uruguay, and Paraguay) in practice increased 71 tariff chapters in Argentina out of 97, in order to harmonize their tariff scheme with Brazil, whose industry strongly favors import substitution.[206] So, while MERCOSUR has been useful in reducing trade barriers among the inefficient four member countries, and thus a tool for regional substitution of imports. Local organizations, such as the Industrial Federation of the State of São Paulo and the Argentine Industrial Union, play a crucial role in shaping the block's policies.

TABLE 10-4
Changes in Import Duties in Argentina
(After the Adoption of MERCOSUR Common Tariff)

	Number of Tariffs
Tariffs Raised	71
Tariffs Unchanged	10
Tariffs Lowered	16
TOTAL	97

Source: This table has been calculated statistically considering the mode (the tariff with highest frequency). Author's figure using data from LAFTA.

Mega protectionism, then, is the main reason an open country like Chile is not a full member of MERCOSUR. Integrating with MERCOSUR would entail disintegration from the rest of the world. Chile's tariff policy (a flat 6 percent) not only prevents distortions in the allocation of resources, but also precludes both group privileges through varying levels of protection as well as corruption opportunities; it is also in sharp contrast with MERCOSUR's wide range of tariff rates (between 0 percent and 35 percent).

The lack of competitiveness of policy making sectors of MERCOSUR has limited progress in signing trade agreements with third parties or trading blocks. Only economic complementation agreements with Chile and Bolivia have gone through, while all other negotiations have stalled due largely to the predominance of protective interests in the local markets over the more competitive exporters, who are generally related to primary markets and farm products.

On the other hand, for Chile, entering into bilateral trade agreements has meant selectively lowering the already low tariff levels. The most notable of these is the recent agreement with the United States, which adds to an already long list of bilateral free trade agreements (Canada, Central America, South Korea, the European Free Trade Association, Mexico, and the European Union) and economic complementation (Bolivia, Colombia, Cuba, Ecuador, MERCOSUR, Peru and Venezuela). In 1994, Chile also became a full member of APEC (Asia Pacific Economic Cooperation).

For Latin America, the rise of non-competitive productive sectors has had long-term negative effects that go beyond the merely economic. When the power of interests snowballs and shapes policies, it becomes harder to confront these interests in order to open up markets. And mega devaluations such as Argentina's in 2002 are applauded because they help close the economy.

The Culture of Unproductive Public Employment

Latin America is characterized by a strong culture of public employment, which in spite of its hypertrophy and lack of productivity, is politically very costly to dismantle.

Historically, public employment was considered a prestigious occupation but one that provided low compensation. For decades, salaries in the public sector trailed the private sector. Only special protections marginally made up for the pay difference. In fact, the very first legal pensions were granted to judges and then to employees in the national judicial system.

Gradually, a substantial institutional change evolved during the twentieth century, as the number of government functions grew, the lobbying power of unions rose, and public funds were allocated according to political goals. The change entailed increases in the quantity of benefits and their duration in time. Public employment was no longer merely prestigious, but now it also carried social benefits whose subsidy would become a heavy burden. Political pretensions came to equate those benefits with social rights. Some constitutions went so far as to incorporate those rights for the whole population, but their origin lies with public employment.

By the middle of the twentieth century, social rights had spread and taken root throughout Latin America, and public employment kept growing. Ministries and agencies that had only a handful of employees earlier in the century ended up with veritable armies of officials, department heads, employees, arranged in complex structures.

The power of unions is one of the main pillars of this system and constitutes one of the premier forces against change in the region. Unions are against public sector reform processes, deregulation of labor markets, and open trade agreements like the FTAA and are fervent demonstrators against globalization. Beyond their romantic and idealistic discourse, they defend tangible interests such as mandatory union contributions that are widespread in Latin America as well as the administration of union health systems as is the case with mandatory contributions to these Union Health Systems in Argentina, sui generis agencies that are neither state nor privately owned, but are union-owned with guaranteed resources and captive markets.

The rigidity of public employment has mortally wounded the quality of services provided by the public sector, which in practice translates into a state which is absent in terms of results, but weighs heavily in the budget. There is an absolute disconnect between the needs of citizens and taxpayers and the effectiveness of the state.

Public employment has taken on a life of its own, regardless of social needs and financing constraints. It generates its own demand. Little has been written about the serious consequences of government-dependent job creation. As time has gone by, perverse institutions have emerged and become engrained, and appear to be culturally stigmatized when it is actually just the logical response to incentives in the legislation.

In the logic of the private sector, to work means to incur effort in order to create value. To create value means to make a good or service that satisfies a need of a person who is in turn willing to pay something for it.

It is only under these circumstances that we can talk of productive work. Any other effort that produces a good or service not valued by others is sterile or unproductive work. In economic terms, value means that somebody is willing to pay something for a product or service.

In the public sector, many officials in ministries and agencies have almost fictitious roles. While they neither add value nor contribute to things getting done in a certain way, those who hold the jobs think they are working productively and put their efforts into what they do. We have turned from work as value creation to work as justification for wages. Regardless of whether or not anything of value is created, the relevant feature of a job is that it is compensated by wages.

With work thus divorced from productivity, there is no clear way to determine, for instance, how many employees are needed to accomplish a goal, be it one, two or ten. What is relevant is the number of salaries that are generated and how many people benefit directly. (On the other hand, it is impossible to quantify the number of those who are indirectly harmed by paying higher taxes or being subjected to stricter regulations).

A corollary of this divorce are the policies of promotions through seniority, salary categories determined by administrative decrees, *enganche* laws,[207] 'kinship' hiring practices,[208] and work rules that ignore productivity considerations. Job pyramids are inverted to the point where there are more managers than rank employees.[209] The salary structure is distorted, and average salary exceeds those in the private sector.

The culture of state interference in the economy is reflected in the educational supply, which responds to the demands of job generating sectors and the aspirations of students considering their vocations. Public employment and the boom in government functions affects career choices, from bachelor degrees to post graduate courses in public administration, to technical degrees specifically tailored to work with regulations. Public accountants, notaries public, government economists, customs brokers, tax experts—all these are specialties born of regulation.

Some university degrees that once aimed at private employment have gradually transformed themselves into virtual centers for public employee applicants. Veterinary and agronomy students are likely to end up in the health and bromatological control offices. Food engineers aspire to control labeling and packaging for public agencies. Thus, regulation creates needs that divert resources away from the educational system.

It is not unusual to hear young people stating their goal of making a career in the public sector. Human resources and education effort are thus diverted from wealth creation in the private sector to regulation in the public sector. With rare exceptions, the entrepreneurial dream is not part of the popular imagery of Latin America.

In summary, the concentrated interests that benefit from redistribution among vested groups block change and reinforce the formal and informal institutions that currently prevail in Latin America.

11
A Way Out for Latin America

This analysis has stressed the important role of institutions and the incentives they create — both on a formal and an informal level — in long-term economic growth. It has demonstrated how the implicit and explicit rules prevailing in a society determine rewards and punishment for individuals and organizations based on whether their behaviors are socially productive or unproductive (although profitable for the acting agent).

The colonization of the American continent in the fifteenth century by two heterogeneous cultures each with their own institutional traditions offers a unique socioeconomic laboratory with two approaches to limiting political power, one from absolutist Spain and one from England on the way to the Glorious Revolution of 1688. Spain had one religion and was on a mission to evangelize the New World; England had seen religious reform. Spain was full of clerical and military hierarchies and privileges; England had developed secular hierarchies. Spain had a command economy aimed at enriching the royal coffers; England was powered by commerce.

The relative importance of the competitive sector to the Crown seems to explain, to a large extent, the rights that the kings were forced to acknowledge. In England, from the thirteenth to the seventeenth centuries the confluence of royal fiscal crises with strong private sectors led the kings to recognize the existence of rights necessary for the development of commercial activity. In Spain, the royal fiscal crises occurred in the context of a lethargic private sector, whose subsistence was tied to the Crown itself, and so, even when the Crown was in trouble, the private sector was not in a position to profit from its weakness.

The short-term result of the rules prevailing in Latin America was that the economy of each country relied on the rents generated by a single mining or agricultural resource. The direct consequence has been the exclusive dependence on the international price of commodities. The single resource was, and in some cases still is, the main source of financing for the public sector, which shared with the private sector the rent-seeking role. The recurring model is one in which the Crown and the State own the resources and private entrepreneurs share the rent derived from exploiting them. A Ricardian analysis can be applied here, including "rents" derived from high productivity of agricultural products, to individual cases in Latin America, such as sugar in Cuba, coffee in Brazil, and even grains in Argentina (1880–1930).

The "rentist" culture of Latin American governments is, in fact, one of the most deep-rooted institutions in the region. The golden age of Spain was built on this institutional basis — and not on an increase in economic productivity. Many have likened the conditions of post-independence Spanish America to a Hobbesian situation, where in the absence of clear ground rules, it was a fight of all against all for survival. It was not until the second half of the 20th century that some consensus — the results of which are still uncertain — was achieved in terms of the rules of alternating power.

Latin America throughout its history has been a rent-seeking society. The phenomenon can partly be explained from the absence of the protection of individual right over democratic mayority control.

The Omnipotent General Will

At the time of their independence, most Latin American countries adopted republican, representative, and federal constitutions based on the Constitution of the United States of America, the first country in the western hemisphere to achieve independence. Despite formal attempts to insert into their constitutions the British institutional framework inherited by the United States, Spanish uses and customs prevailed over the new formal rules.

The Constitution of the United States embodied traditions that were alien to Latin America. Its main objective was to place limits on the arbitrariness of the State and defend the inalienable rights of citizens, a goal clearly consistent with the ideas of John Locke and other empiricists like David Hume and Adam Ferguson. Locke's position was that the government came to be in order to protect pre-existing rights, and if it abuses those rights, it contradicts its very essence; government exists to put an end to the private and subjective application of justice, replacing it with a contract whose independent rules allows more certainty in the observation of individual rights.

Thus, the "social contract" that gives rise to government aims to protect natural rights—to life, liberty, and property—of individuals. Locke defined the power that citizens granted to the government as a "political trusteeship," that is a limited power entrusted for a single purpose. Consistent with this, he also recognized the right of citizens to rebel against abusive governments that violate the essence of that contract.

For some authors such as Marcel Prelot,[210] "voting with one's feet"—as embodied by the British citizens who traveled to the new world to found the original thirteen colonies that would become the United States—represents an explicit instance of adhesion to a new social contract in the manner described by Locke.

The writings of John Locke supported a limited democracy, in which the only role of government is the protection of individual rights, and, in this sense, represented the foundation for the British *Glorious Revolution* of 1688 as well as the guiding spirit of the republic of the United States of America.

This institutional and historical legacy is alien to Latin American countries at the time of their independence. As we saw in Chapter 4, the absolutism of the crown was substituted for the power of omnipotent *caudillos*, whose quasi feudal practices in their areas of influence allowed the old political culture to live on.

Armando Ribas writes that "the rule of law"—the basic organizational principle of the society of the United States—was disregarded or even denigrated widely in continental Europe and Latin America; and adds that the rule of law is the antithesis of the Reason of State, in which a majority prevails over the rights of individuals. Ribas goes on to comment that Latin America is the land of rational obscurantism, where individual rights are disregarded, in favor of so-called human rights. The latter comprise social rights, which are nothing more than government-granted privileges, ignoring the "rule of law."[211]

Just as Locke represented the spirit of the Glorious Revolution and the American Revolution, Jean Jacques Rousseau embodied the values of the French Revolution of 1789, in particular through his concept of the "general will" which is revealed through the voice of the majority. According to this doctrine, writes Prelot, when the majority has spoken, those in the minority must accept that truth is in the will as determined by the majority.[212]

Immanuel Kant, like Rousseau, believed that rights did not precede but rather arise from the constitution of the State, and wrote that men completely abandoned their savage and illegal freedom with the goal of finding a true freedom and not a state of legal dependency, because this dependency is created by their own legislative free will. According to Ribas, Kant could not grasp the nature of the political system created by the constitution of the United States, where the Supreme Court held and still holds the power to resist and restrict or limit abuses of the law both by the executive and the legislative branches.[213]

The French Revolution of 1789 had the goal of putting an end to the arbitrariness of kings and the tremendous tax burden on the population, but brought about the reign of terror and the execution of close to 40,000 people. The years that ensued witnessed staggering inflation, war, chaos, and ended with the first police state, under Napoleon. Following the Revolution, government became highly centralized. The administration by the king was replaced with the National Assembly.

In "A Tale of Two Revolutions,"[214] Robert Peterson highlights the profound differences between the French and the American Revolutions. He writes that although on the surface there are some parallels between the two, the bloodless revolution of the United States is much closer to the Glorious Revolution of 1688, while the French has been considered the antecedent to many violent revolutions that have given rise to totalitarian and dictatorial regimes.

And while in France religious dissidents were executed, religious freedom was one of the basic tenets of the United States. The Constitutional Convention of 1787 was attended by devout Congregationalists, Dutch Reformists, Lutherans, Quakers, Presbyterians, Methodists, and roman Catholics.

Peterson adds that the American Revolution was in essence a conservative movement that fought to preserve the freedoms it had attained in 1620 during the period of "salutary neglect." Samuel Eliot Morison writes that the American Revolution was not a fight for freedom but one to preserve the liberties that the American colonies enjoyed. Freedom was not a conscious end in itself but a means to preserve life, liberty, and the pursuit of happiness.[215]

The 19th century French economist, Frederic Bastiat wrote that the French Revolution failed because it repudiated the principles on which a free society rests: self-government, private property, free markets, and limited government. On the other hand, the American Revolution brought about the freest society in the world. In Bastiat's words:

> Look at the United States. There is no country in the world where the law confines itself more rigorously to its proper role, which is to

> guarantee everyone's liberty and property. Accordingly, there is no country in which the social order seems to rest on a more stable foundation.... This is how they understand freedom and democracy in the United States. There each citizen is vigilant with a jealous care to remain his own master. It is by virtue of such freedom that the poor hope to emerge from poverty, and that the rich hope to preserve their wealth. And, in fact, as we see, in a very short time this system has brought the Americans to a degree of enterprise, security, wealth, and equality of which the annals of the human race offer no other example.... [In America] each person can in full confidence dedicate his capital and his labor to production. He does not have to fear that his plans and calculations will be upset from one instant to another by the legislature.[216]

In Europe and Latin America, history has shown that the superiority of the interests of the majority over the rights of individuals permitted the emergence of totalitarian regimes in Europe, and authoritarian regimes (under democratic or non-democratic forms) in Latin America. The emergence of Adolf Hitler's nazism within a system of democratic elections by the majority rule is a clear example of the dangers of democracies based on the general will.

The progressive "democratization" that the region underwent in the 1980s was characterized by free elections with officials elected by the majority rule, a system more in tune with the values of the French Revolution than with the spirit of the United States revolution, that is to say, one that is closer to Jean Jacques Rousseau's general will than to John Locke's limited government.

Thus, we find two types of democracies: one where individual rights precede and have priority over existence of government; and one in which rights exist as a consequence of the social contract and are subordinate to the general will.

About these two traditions, Armando Ribas writes that it was not in continental Europe where the basic tenets of capitalism were born. That is, the moral acceptance of private interests, the legal recognition of individual rights, the limitation of political power as a consequence of the fallibility of human nature, the limits of reason and the right of each individual to pursue their own happiness. This North American vision was imposed or accepted by Western Europe during the Cold War for fear of the Soviets and due to North American protection. Ever since the Fall of the Berlin Wall, however, old cultural characteristics have re-emerged both in Eastern and in Western Europe.[217]

This rules framework is the ideal background for the emergence of populist and redistributive regimes that generate uncertainty and submit the legislative and judicial branches to their voracity. In this context, the power to legislate falls on the population, its power comes from the people and all rules are necessarily "fair." Here, as in the Rousseauian worldview, individual rights do not precede but are derived from civil government. This criterion, which prevails in Latin American societies, has been an open door for abuses of power even within democratic frameworks, where the Supreme Court tends to act as an accomplice to political power rather than a defender of constitutional rights.

Thus, the stability of the rules of society in the region depends on the will of presidents who wield highly concentrated power, even within the boundaries of democracy. The failure of market-oriented reforms in democratic environments in Argentina, Bolivia, and Venezuela are clear instances of this.

The young Latin American democracies represent complicated situations, where legitimacy rests on the majority rule and where respect for individual rights is an afterthought. It has not proved easy to implement and cement rules which are consistent with an informal tradition altogether foreign to the existing framework.

Centralism as an Unshakable Legacy

Economically, centralism is a "policy failure," inefficiently allocating the economic resources of citizens and producing noise between the demands of consumer-voters and producer-politicians. Research by FIEL (Fundación de Investigaciones Económicas Latinoamericanas) finds that decentralization of responsibilities brings taxpayers and voters closer to public decision making. More decentralized governments lead to the consolidation of genuine democracy. This is also consistent with the principles of competition, efficiency, and decentralization of economic, political, and union power.[218]

The same research finds that incentives for orderly and socially convenient behavior have been adulterated in centralist societies. It is an accepted practice to maximize public spending with the purpose of bestowing subsidies on a few. The pressure to spend more resulted in another practice: transferring the responsibility of financing additional expenditures to other jurisdictions. The separation between the decision to spend and the obligation to pay created enormous system-wide inefficiencies.[219]

TABLE 11-1
Comparison of the Two Institutional Legacies

	Latin America	United States
Fiscal correspondence	No	Yes
Political responsibility	Diffuse	Direct
Electoral system	-Party list -Voting is mandatory -Party discipline	-Individual candidate by district -Voting is voluntary -Ideology discipline
Competition between political parties	Monopolistic or with serious barriers to entry	Competitive, open to individuals running
Administration of public goods	Centralized, national or provincial	Decentralized, local level
Law Enforcement	National and provincial police chiefs	Sheriffs elected by citizenry
Role of municipalities and counties	Minor, last stage in political parties	First stepping stone in growth within political parties priorities of citizens

TABLE 11-2
The Spanish Antecedents of the Reforms of the 1990s

Area	Spanish Antecedents to the reforms	Latin America During 1990s	The Future of Latin America — Without Real Reform
Justice system	Secondary role Subject to political power	Secondary role Second generation reforms Dependent on political power	Dependent on political power More interference with the Judiciary
Trade	Free trade between hub and colonies, and among colonies	Trade managed through closed blocks	Hardening of trade blocks Deviation of trade Regional isolation
Privatizations	Capitulaciones: The Crown contracts with private groups for a limited time of concessions	State contracts out to private monopolies Markets highly regulated	More regulation Larger role of the State More redistribution of rents
Public spending	Growing, financed through revenue from natural resources	Growing, financed through debt	Growing, with financing problems Crisis

In addition, James Buchanan wrote that the reason his normative theory of competitive federalism is congenial to economists is that it is an extension of the principles of market economy to the organization of the political structure.[220] The market economy produces high levels of value that benefit all participants; individuals have legally protected rights to enter and leave production and exchange relationships. Federalism offers a mechanism to introduce the main elements of the market into politics. Federalism serves two purposes: it allows for the reduction of the role of the central government and, simultaneously, limits the potential for provinces (or states) to exploit citizens.

Is There an End to the Latin American Vicious Cycle?

Latin America has enjoyed periods of economic growth, which eventually proved not to be lasting, among them in Argentina (1880–1930), Mexico (from Porfirio Díaz until 1917), Chile (República Portalina), Brazil (1964–1985). More recently — end of the 1980s and early 1990s — Argentina, Chile, Mexico, Peru, etc., have experienced a change in economic performance, powered by some changes in the formal rules. These changes have been undone in Argentina, Peru, Bolivia and Venezuela in the 2000's by the persistent lack of legal security and protection of private property rights.

Although the processes known as the "1990s Latin American economic reforms" were appealing compared to the stagnation of previous decades, they did not observe certain rules that are the bases of republics. The reforms did not respect private property, the division of power, nor the constitutional order, as attested by the experiences in Argentina, Peru, Bolivia, Ecuador, Venezuela, and more recently, Brazil.

In his theory of institutional change, Douglass North writes that institutional change from less to more efficient stems from the perception of entrepreneurs— both economic and political — and organizations in a society that there are opportunities for potential new rules of the game that would be more beneficial to their own interests. Implicit in this statement is the notion that in a process of change there will be "winners" and "losers." A simple example would be the non–competitive industrial groups that oppose opening the economy, where more competitive participants would defend the possibility. Industrial groups, unions and politicians form a solid block for continuing to have a closed economy with privileges distributed to maintain power.

Friedrich von Hayek studied how limitations on political power liberate individual energies which, pursuing their own ends through trial and error, create spontaneous institutions such as language, money, insurance, bills of exchange, corporations, etc., and today, credit cards and the Internet. In the absence of restrictions, those institutions that have proven more efficient should replace — at least partially — the least efficient ones, for instance, tractors should replace manual plowing, credit cards paper money, electronic mail traditional mail, etc. But in fact, this institutional convergence is delayed precisely because those who were winners under the old system will always attempt to prevent change.

Among the results of the recent Latin American reforms appears that the old power groups have blocked the reforms that were put in place and are moving toward the rent seeking economy (except Chile).

What Guarantees That the Reforms Will Last?

Notwithstanding the critical eye this book casts on the history of Latin American institutions, recent signs allows to be pessimistic towards a change in the rules of the game even though exogenous pressures are being brought to bear on these nations by globalization.

There is some external pressure arising from the needs for foreign financing to cover budget deficits. In some instances, trade agreements between countries act as a constraint on foreign policies (on raising tariffs, on devaluing the exchange rate, etc.) and condition how foreign investments are treated. Competition to attract investments to Latin America has diminished because of disruptions in Argentina, Colombia, Venezuela, Peru, Ecuador and to certain extent Brazil due to the lack of respect for property rights.

For the purposes of this book, the globalization process can be seen as the growing interconnectedness among hitherto economically isolated countries. As information flows across borders, and the remaining walls around nations weaken, apparently unrelated events lead to changes in the rules. Just as the increased productivity of the Industrial Revolution led to a profound social and economic reorganization, the growing interconnection of the world economy has undeniable effects on institutional rules.

New and powerful economic relationships will bring rewards and punishments even in countries with the institutions and rules most unfavorable to economic growth. Pressures generated by "globalization" can break down the strongest rent-seeking coalitions. Greater accessibility to information has already exposed the inflated costs of goods and services in countries that maintain restrictions such as bans or quotas on imports. This exposure puts pressure on those governments to, at the very least, search for more sophisticated arguments to justify their perverse policies.

Countries with the least efficient rules may stand to benefit most from globalization. In spite of the formally democratic regimes in Latin America, there is a considerable gap between their reality and the ideals described by Montesquieu or the reality in countries like the United States or the United Kingdom. In Latin America, globalization pressures are in conflict with the powerful interests that traditionally have had the authority to allocate political and economic privileges arbitrarily.

Significant institutional changes are required to end poverty and stagnation:

INDEPENDENCE OF THE JUDICIARY

Clear rules are required for protecting individual right over majority control. An independent judicial power to exercise a judicial review over the legislative and executive power is essential if these rights are to be up herded. The constitutional principle of an independent judicial power must be enforced to establish the mechanisms for the protection of the individual rights against the advances of the government. Judges must be selected by a magisterial council with public debate of the credentials of potential candidates. The restitution of independence and the pursuit of higher efficiency is a *sine qua non* prerequisite for the market to function correctly.

CHANGES IN POLITICAL SYSTEMS

The market process can only function on the basis of an adequate institutional framework, and the fundamental institutional reforms are yet to begin a modern system of election of public officials, and a transparent mechanism for financing political parties.

The system of rewards and punishments implied in commercial and civil competition must be applied to the political sphere. Accountability for elected officials can be achieved through single candidate electoral systems. Knowing one's representatives will give voters a natural control, more powerful than any audit or commission entrusted to do so. Voting for individual candidates at the lowest possible levels of decentralized government will yield better and more honest elected officials. The elimination of party lists is essential for elective offices to be filled by able, honest, and truly representative citizens. To eliminate the monopoly by political parties it is essential for the political system to be open to outsiders. The current and obscure way of financing political parties should be replaced with transparent alternatives that prevent campaign contributions from being used to obtain privileges and protections of any sort. It is also imperative to use the voting mechanism to elect those responsible for the provision of basic local services, such as police, hospitals, schools and firemen.

Taxation

Latin America is a poor region, whose resources have been wasted and misallocated for many decades; it cannot support an overextended state. The highest growth rates in the history of the region occurred in the years when government intervention and its role were reduced, and so redefining the role of the state implies reducing its functions and its size. When voters will benefit from public spending increases but do not have to shoulder the burden of financing them, they have no incentive to oppose increases in state expenditure. To ensure public support for fiscal restraint, many countries maintain a close link between the ability to tax and the responsibility for spending, even when collecting at a higher level of government might prove more efficient.

Fiscal correspondence has the additional advantage of clearly establishing the relative price of tax-public expenditure, that is, the marginal fiscal pressure faced by taxpayers is tied to an adequate provision of services. Given the scarcity of resources, the higher public spending, the lower the private spending, or in other words, the lower the remuneration for productive factors, like labor and land. Taxation must revert to local and provincial governments including income tax.

Education

Education can be a catalyst for new habits and values. The current global environment requires education curricula that can be adjusted to new realities. Education decentralization at the municipal level is a must under a public financed education system. Such a system — although free in the early stages— must include competitive mechanisms for quality and control of management. Current proposals, such as a system of educational vouchers or parent-run schools, must be implemented to stimulate price mechanisms in education. Although the results from educational reform are long term and take many years to materialize, they are a key element in the consolidation of a new framework of societal rules.

Federalism and the Elimination of National Functions

The provision of public goods by the state must be carried out in the most decentralized manner possible. Education, health, security and some functions of justice — must be provided exclusively at municipal levels of government voting locally must improve quality, cost and competitive mechanism to having more efficient and effective public services. Redundant national functions must be eliminated and budgetary and regulatory duplication avoided.

Open Trade

Opening all domestic markets and participating in the international trade boom will allow the influx of competitive habits. Replacing public employment and government activity with commerce and productive activities will encourage innovation and respect for property rights. Closed trading blocks — where the generalized benefits of trading with the world are replaced with the benefits to some groups of trading with a few relatively less efficient economies — are a threat to open economies. The integration agreements signed by Latin American countries (Mercosur, Pacto Andino, Comunidad de los Tres, Caricom, etc.) represent obstacles to the continued reduction of tariffs and trade restrictions.

Privatization and Deregulation of Closed Markets

In spite of the privatization processes undertaken in Latin America, in several countries there still exist entire sectors of the economies that are private or state monopolies such as state-provided services in Uruguay, oil in Venezuela and Mexico, all hinder the development of new institutions and are sources of unproductive rents.

Identifying and Eliminating Subsidies and Rents

All the countries in the region have special regimes for selected industries or for encouraging the development of specific geographical areas. These include explicit and implicit subsidies, public employment opportunities, and special economic development schemes. These are, in fact, unproductive rents, but more importantly they are the seeds of unproductive habits. The areas in Latin America reliant on public subsidy range from the poorest to the most powerful industrial regions. In the case of industries or companies, their pleas for low interest loans or tax exemptions are a means to obtain benefits by taxing other productive activities.

Control of Currency

The constitutional control of debt and the incorporation of a truly independent Central Bank through a convertible scheme that allows Central Bank to issue currency when exports are made and contract currency when imports are required.

Globalization

External factors (trade boom, low transaction costs, internationalization of production and markets) condition institutional change. These systems consist of respect of private property rights, free movement of factors of production, and economic and legal stability. To take full advantage of global trade, Latin America must have stable rules of the game if it wants to gain in the trade game.

Conclusion

Many of the so-called reforms were nothing but a modern version of *capitulaciones*—documents through which the Spanish Crown had permitted the exploitation of their territories in the Indies. In fact, similarities are striking between the *capitulaciones* and modern day privatizations as implemented in Latin America. In neither case is there a transfer of title; both institutions keep the state as the true owner, with the licensee having the right to use. Both institutions also involve the protection of the market through regulatory mechanisms (prices, investments, etc.) that limit or altogether preclude competition. In both cases, the government acts to redistribute rents.

Internationally, the much-promoted opening of the economy has been nothing but a lighter version of "managed trade" achieved through regional agreements. The intent to trade freely with all countries in the world was precluded by the establishment of closed trading blocks, which amount to an expanded protectionism. Indeed, trade barriers that in previous decades isolated countries in the region now isolate blocks. International trade figures for the countries in question show higher growth among "natural partners" than with the rest of the world. This supports the argument that, far from creating more trade opportunities and expanding competition, blocks close markets and divert trade. Mercosur, the Comunidad Andina (formerly Pacto Andino), and the endless bilateral agreements under ALADI show that the countries in the region do not intend to trade with the world but to open markets slightly without risking international competition.

Monetary stability has been maintained with the help of foreign financing. The rate of inflation was reduced (in Argentina, Peru, Brazil, and Bolivia) by reorganizing public financing rather than by curtailing public spending, which in fact grew. Instead of reducing spending to the basic functions of government (justice, security, and social services), the countries in the region replaced inflationary financing with public debt.

The public debt grew *pari passu* with the increase in public spending. What had previously been financed through inflation was now being financed through more debt and through higher taxes. Although it is true that genuine sources of fiscal revenue (taxation) are less traumatic than spurious financing (issuing currency), it is equally true that high levels of public expenditure — regardless of how they are financed — hurt productivity in the private sector. In turn, if companies go bankrupt and there is a crisis in the balance of payments, it becomes harder to support high levels of expenditure.

Ultimately, the application of public expenditure and political power to redistribute rents among private individuals is a practice — almost an informal institution — that continues to grow.

Political systems with monopolistic political parties, electoral systems with party lists, and no controls over campaign finance have established a political "corporation" with privileges, tax exemptions, early and generous retirement, and special immunities and constitutes a source of rents for the larger and most influential private organized groups.

Instead of operating within the rules of markets and satisfying the demands of customers, these interest groups realize it is more profitable to walk the corridors of public agencies and try to obtain subsidies and protections against competitors. It is easier to extract benefits from the government than to earn a living serving the customer by producing the best goods and services.

Anticompetitive behaviors so common in Latin America thrive in systems in which public expenditure is unchecked, political power is centralized, and there are no constraints on the actions of government.

Despite multiple reform attempts in Latin America, resistance to changing old rules of the game has proved surprisingly strong, stemming mainly from the direct beneficiaries of the status quo, from redistributive cultural values, and from a system of positive laws that have served the purposes of populist governments. The foundations of the current stability are weak. Only superficial changes have been achieved so far. The strength of these traditions was evident in the retreat from the timid market-oriented reforms in countries such as Argentina, Venezuela, Colombia, Peru, Ecuador, among others. This is why these are not reforms in the real sense of the word.

An effective attack on poverty in Latin America will come only when its deep causes are understood. Among the essential elements of a successful approach will be the reconstruction of the republics with a separate independent judicial review power to protect individual rights.

At the beginning of the twenty-first century, democracy in Latin America is conceived as the government of the majority, with an executive power that acts with complete disregard for individual rights. The absence of an autonomous judicial branch to protect constitutional rights opens the door to a redistributive society that offers few incentives for productive behaviors. This will be the beginning of the end of poverty and stagnation in Latin America.

Notes

1. Douglass C. North, *Institutions, Institutional Change and Economic performance*, Cambridge University Press, Cambridge, 1990, p. 107.
2. Guillermo M. Yeatts, *Subsurface Wealth: The Struggle for Privatization in Argentina*, The Foundation for Economic Education, Inc. (FEE), Irvington-on-Hudson, 1997.
3. The image of oil discovery creating instant millionaires is part of popular culture in the United States, captured in idiom and even forming the premise of a 1970s television series.
4. Arthur Shenfield, "Hayek y el derecho," *Libertas* 7, ESEADE, Buenos Aires (October 1987): 106ff.
5. *Ibid.*, p. 108.
6. José I. García Hamilton, *El autoritarismo hispanoamericano y la improductividad*, Editorial Sudamericana, Buenos Aires, 1998.
7. Mariano Grondona, *Las condiciones culturales del desarrollo económico. Hacia una teoría del desarrollo*, Editorial Planeta, Buenos Aires, 1999; Lawrence E. Harrison, *El sueño panamericano*, Editorial Ariel, Buenos Aires, 1999 and *El subdesarrollo está en la mente: el caso latinoamericano*, 1985.
8. Carlos Montaner, et al., *Fabricantes de miseria*, Plaza & Janés, Barcelona, 1998.
9. Paul Craig Roberts and Karen Lafollette Araujo, *The Capitalist Revolution in Latin America*, Oxford University Press, New York, 1997.
10. North, op. cit., Preface, p. vii.
11. North and Thomas, *The Rise of the Western World. A New Economic History*, Cambridge University Press, Cambridge, 1976.
12. David Rock, *Argentina 1516–1982 From Spanish Colonization to the Falklands War*, University of California Press, Los Angeles and Berkeley, 1985, p. xxv.
13. Friedrich von Hayek, *Law, Legislation and Liberty.*
14. Even the economic reforms of the 1990s—which many consider a turning point in institutional terms—were fueled by serious fiscal crises that led governments to shed unprofitable public corporations and increase the value of depreciated assets by enacting statutory restrictions to competition.
15. Gordon Tullock, "The Backward Society: Static Inefficiency, Rent Seeking and The Rule of Law," in *The Theory of Public Choice II*, The University of Michigan, Ann Arbor, 1994, p. 224.
16. Frederic Bastiat, *The Law*, The Foundation for Economic Education, Inc. (FEE), Irvington-on-Hudson, New York, 1950, pp. 12–13.
17. Hernando de Soto, *The Other Path*, Harper & Row, Publishers, New York, 1989, Foreword by Mario Vargas Llosa, pp. xviii–xix.
18. John Locke, *Two Treatises of Government*, Cambridge University Press, Cambridge, 1988.
19. Jaime Vicens Vives, *An Economic History of Spain*, Princeton University Press, Princeton, 1969, p. 294.
20. Douglass North, *Institutions, Institutional Change and Economic Performance*, p. 130.
21. Octavio Paz, *The Labryinth of Solitude and Other Writings*, New York: Grove Press, 1985, p. 361.
22. *Ibid.*
23. José I. García Hamilton, op. cit., p. 58.
24. We should note that Pope John Paul II apologized publicly in the name of the Catholic Church for the case of Galileo, some excesses in the Conquest of America, the treatment of Jews, and the Inquisition (see Luigi Accattoli, *Mea Culpa*, Editorial Grijalbo, Barcelona, 1998).

25. Octavio Paz, op. cit., pp. 360–61.
26. Douglass C. North, op. cit., p. 114.
27. Ibid.
28. Norberto Gorostiaga, *Recurso extraordinario ante la Corte Suprema de la Nación: orígenes históricos,* Buenos Aires, 1944, p. 71.
29. William P. Glade, *The Latin American Economies: A Study of Their Institutional Evolution,* American Book, New York, 1969, p. 58.
30. Jan De Vries, *The Economy in Europe in an Age of Crisis, 1600–1750,* Cambridge University Press, Cambridge, 1976, p. 28.
31. J. D. Elliot, "The Decline of Spain," *Past and Present* 20 (November 1961): 87.
32. North, op. cit., p. 115.
33. Ibid., p. 113.
34. Ibid., p. 116.
35. A. V. Dicey, *Introduction to the Study of the Law of the Constitution,* MacMillan and Company, New York, 1961, p. 1.
36. Ricardo M. Rojas, "El orden jurídico espontáneo," *Libertas* 13, ESEADE, Buenos Aires (October 1990): 198.
37. Oliver Wendell Holmes, Jr., *The Common Law,* Little, Brown and Company, Boston, 1938, p. 1.
38. Chalmers and Hood Phillips, *Constitutional Laws of Great Britain, the British Empire and the Commonwealth,* 6th edition, Sweet and Maxwell Ltd., London, 1946, p. 10.
39. Charles Borgeaud, *Établissement et révision des constitutions en Amérique et en Europe,* Ed. Thorin et Fils, Paris, 1893, p. 6.
40. This comparison is based on the one the author developed for *Subsurface Wealth.*
41. North, p. 117.
42. Friedrich A. Hayek, *Inflación o pleno empleo,* Union Editorial, Madrid, 1976, p. 183. Quoted in María Gabriela Mrad, "El *common law* en la tradición del orden espontáneo," *Libertas* 12, ESEADE, (May 1990), p. 138.
43. That same year European Calvinism was endangered with the revocation of the Edict of Nantes, granted in 1598 by Henry IV of France for the protection of Protestants in the country. The result of the revocation was the persecution of the Protestants and the strengthening of the absolute power of kings by divine right, the very position that James II held in England.
44. John Locke, op. cit.
45. John Locke, op. cit.
46. John Locke, op. cit.
47. George H. Sabine, *Historia de la teoría política* (Spanish translation by Vicente Herrero), Fondo de Cultura Económica, Mexico, 1963, p. 267.

48. Raymond G. Gettel, *Political Science,* Vol. 1, Ginn and Co., Boston, 1949, p. 247.
49. Martin Luther, *De la libertad del hombre cristiano.* Quoted in Linares Quintana, op. cit., p. 512.
50. Anthony Guiddens, in the Foreword to Max Weber, *The Protestant Ethic and the Spirit of Capitalism,* George Allen & Unwin Ltd., London, 1976, p. 3.
51. Paz, op. cit., p. 365.
52. Ibid., p. 369.
53. Luis Roque Gondra, *Estudios de historia y economía,* Imprenta de la Universidad, Buenos Aires, 1938, p. 109.
54. Eric Roll, *Historia de las doctrinas económicas,* Fondo de Cultura Económica, Mexico, 1994, p. 44.
55. Ibid., p. 44.
56. Gondra, op. cit., p. 110.
57. Ibid., p. 111.
58. Jorge E. Bustamante, *Desregulación. Entre el derecho y la economía,* Abeledo Perrot, Buenos Aires, 1993, pp. 41–2.
59. Douglass C. North, op. cit., p. 125.
60. Robert S. López, and Irving W. Raymond, *Medieval Trade in the Mediterranean,* Columbia University Press, New York, 1955, p. 163. Quoted in North, p. 125.
61. Florence E. De Roover, "Early Examples of Marine Insurance," *Journal of Economic History* 5: 198.
62. William Mitchell, *An Essay on the Early History of the Law Merchant,* Burt Franklin Press, New York, 1969, p. 156. Quoted in Douglass North, op. cit., p. 127.
63. Juan B Alberdi, *Escritos póstumos,* Universidad Nacional de Quilmes, Buenos Aires, 1996, p. 96.
64. José I. García Hamilton, op. cit., pp. 43, 47.
65. Juan B. Alberdi, op. cit., p. 88.
66. Oreste Popescu, *Studies in the History of Latin American Thought,* Routledge, London and New York, 1997, p. 82.
67. Alberto M. Salas, *Las armas de la conquista,* Emecé Editores, Buenos Aires, 1950, p. 5.
68. Ibid., p. 7.
69. Hernán Cortés, *Cartas,* p. 17, cited in Alberto M. Salas, op. cit., p. 9.
70. García Hamilton, op. cit., pp. 45–46.
71. Ione S.Wright and Lisa M. Nekhom, *Diccionario histórico argentino,* Emecé Editores, Buenos Aires, 1990, p. 225.
72. Oreste Popescu, *Studies in the History of Latin American Thought,* Routledge, London and New York, 1997, p. 89.

73. *Ibid.*, Popescu, pp. 89–90.
74. *Ibid.*, p. 90.
75. *Ibid.*, Popescu, p. 87.
76. *Ibid.*, Oreste Popescu, *Studies in the History of Latin American Thought*, Routledge, London and New York, 1997, pp. 89–90.
77. Octavio Paz, op. cit., p. 144.
78. John H. Coatsworth, "Obstacles to Economic Growth in Nineteenth Century Mexico," *American Historical Review* 83 (1978): 94.
79. Roberto T. Alemann, *Breve historia de la política económica argentina 1500–1989*, Editorial Claridad, Buenos Aires, 1990, p. 15.
80. David Rock, *Argentina 1516–1982 from Spanish Colonization to the Falklands War*, University of California Press, Los Angeles and Berkeley, 1985, pp. 14–15.
81. *Ibid.*
82. Ione S. Wright and Lisa M. Nekhom, op. cit., p. 160.
83. Tulio Halperín Donghi, *Historia contemporánea de América latina*, Alianza Editorial, Buenos Aires, 1994, pp. 18–19.
84. Harold U. Faulkner, *American Economic History*, Harpers and Brothers Publishers, New York and London, 1935, p. 47.
85. *Ibid.* The author adds, "This attitude is well expressed in the remonstrance of the company to the States-General against a peace with Spain, when they maintained that their object was not 'trifling trade with the Indians nor the tardy cultivation of uninhabited regions,' but 'acts of hostility against the ships and property of the King of Spain and his subjects'" (p .47).
86. *Ibid.*, pp. 49–50.
87. Jorge Cárdenas Nannetti, *Los Estados Unidos, ayer y hoy*, Grupo Editorial Norma, Buenos Aires, 1998, p. 35.
88. Harold U. Faulkner, op. cit., p. 69.
89. Jorge Cárdenas Nannetti, op. cit., p. 63.
90. Harold U. Faulkner, op. cit., p. 70.
91. John Lynch, *The Spanish American Revolutions, 1808–1826*, Norton, New York, 1986, p. 1.
92. *Ibid.*, p. 7.
93. *Ibid.*, p. 2.
94. *Ibid.*, p. 138.
95. *Ibid.*, p. 139.
96. *Ibid.*, p. 140.
97. Claudio Véliz, *The Centralist Tradition of Latin America*, Princeton University Press, Princeton, 1982, pp. 144ff.
98. Charles C. Griffin, "The Enlightment and Latin American Independence," in *Latin America and the Enlightment*, p. 138, cited by Claudio Véliz, op. cit., p. 154.
99. José I. García Hamilton, op. cit., pp. 153ff.
100. William P. Glade, op. cit., p. 185.
101. Roberto Cortés Conde, *Progreso y declinación de la economía argentina*, Fondo de Cultura Económica, Buenos Aires, 1998, p. 14.
102. *Ibid.*, p. 16.
103. Tulio Halperín Donghi, op. cit., p. 146.
104. *Ibid.*, p. 136.
105. *Ibid.*, pp. 146ff.
106. Quoted in Samuel Morison, Henry Commager, and William Leuchtenburg, *A Concise History of the American Republic*, Oxford University Press, New York, 1977, p. 97.
107. *Ibid.*, p. 132.
108. *Ibid.*, p. 133.
109. *Ibid.*
110. Samuel Morison, Henry Commager, and William Leuchtenburg, op. cit., p. 228.
111. Anti-Federalist Paper No. 1, "General Introduction: A Dangerous Plan of Benefit only to the Aristocratic Combination."
112. Samuel Morison, Henry Commager, and William Leuchtenburg, op. cit., p. 251–52.
113. Anti Federalist Paper No. 1, "General Introduction: A Dangerous Plan of Benefit only to the Aristocratic Combination," October 18, 1787.
114. *Ibid.*
115. George Clinton quoted in Alberto Benegas Lynch (h), "Los papeles Antifederalistas," *Libertas* 10, ESEADE, Buenos Aires (May 1989), p. 244.
116. Claudio Véliz, op. cit., pp. 3ff.
117. *Ibid.*, pp. 147–151.
118. J. Lloyd Mecham, *Church and State in Latin America: A History of Politico-Ecclesiastical Relations*, Chapel Hill, N.C., 1966, p. 164, quoted by Claudio Véliz, op. cit., p. 155.
119. Juan B. Alberdi, *Sistema económico y rentístico de la Confederación Argentina según su Constitución de 1853*, Editorial Raigal, Buenos Aires, 1954, p. 53.
120. William P. Glade, op. cit., p. 175.
121. *Ibid.*, p. 212.
122. Tulio Halperín Donghi, op. cit., p. 195.
123. *Ibid.*, p. 192.
124. Roberto Cortés Conde, op. cit., p. 23.
125. William Glade, op. cit., p. 213.
126. Tulio Halperín Donghi, op. cit., p. 201.
127. *Ibid.*, p. 201.
128. William Glade, op. cit., p. 216.
129. *Ibid.*, p. 216.
130. Roberto Cortés Conde, op. cit., p. 20.
131. William Glade, op. cit., p. 213.
132. *Ibid.*, p. 196.
133. Douglass C. North, op. cit., p. 133.

134. Roberto Cortés Conde, op. cit., p. 12.
135. William P. Glade, op. cit., p. 186.
136. Ibid., p. 101, 103.
137. Ibid., p. 92.
138. Ibid.
139. Charles Rawley, "Institutional Choice and Public Choice," in *The Revolution in Development Economics*, The Cato Institute, Washington, D.C., 1998.
140. Juan José Llach, *Otro siglo, otra Argentina*, Editorial Ariel, Buenos Aires, 1997, p. 19.
141. Charles Rawley, op. cit.
142. Pablo A. Ramella, *Derecho constitucional*, Ediciones Depalma, Buenos Aires, 1986.
143. Ibid., p. 402.
144. Maurice Duverger, *Instituciones políticas y derecho constitucional*, Editorial Ariel, Barcelona, 1984, pp. 598ff.
145. Hernando de Soto, *The Other Path. The Invisible Revolution in the Third World*, Foreword by Mario Vargas Llosa, Perennial Library, New York, 1990, pp. xviii–xix.
146. Jan Kñákal y Aníbal Pinto, "El sistema centro-periferia 20 años después," in *Economía internacional y desarrollo. Estudios en honor de Raúl Prebisch*, Ediciones Depalma, Buenos Aires, 1974.
147. CEPAL, *Estudio Económico de América Latina, 1949*, New York, 1951.
148. Luis E.Di Marco, "Pensamiento económico de Prebisch," in *Economía internacional...*, op. cit.
149. Eduardo Galeano, *Las venas abiertas de América Latina*, Editorial del Chanchito, Montevideo, 1996.
150. Jan Kñákal and Aníbal Pinto, op. cit., p. 106.
151. Fernando Henrique Cardoso, "Desarrollo y dependencia: Perspectivas teóricas en el análisis sociológico," in *Sociología del desarrollo*, Ediciones Solar, Buenos Aires, 1970.
152. Juan M.Vacchino, *Integración Latinoamericana. De la ALALC a la ALADI*, Ediciones Depalma, Buenos Aires, 1983, p. 34.
153. Ibid., p. 51.
154. Eduardo Galeano, op. cit., pp. 14ff.
155. Norberto Bobbio and Nicola Matteucci, *Diccionario de ciencia política*, Siglo XXI Editores, Mexico, 1986.
156. John J. Johnson, *Militares y sociedad en América latina*, Ediciones Solar-Hachette S.A., Buenos Aires, 1966, pp. 147ff.
157. Ibid., p. 147.
158. Alfred Stepan, *Rethinking Military Politics: Brazil and the Southern Cone*, Princeton University Press, Princeton, 1988, p. 80.
159. Maurice Duverger, op. cit., p. 601.

160. Juan Carlos Casas, *Nuevos políticos y nuevas políticas en América latina*, Editorial Atlántida, Buenos Aires, 1991, p. 14.
161. Ibid., p. 24.
162. Juan José Llach, op. cit., p. 66.
163. Enrique Szewach, "El Estado quedó obligado a emitir permanentemente," in *Ámbito Financiero*, February 1990.
164. Roberto Cortés Conde, op. cit., p. 115.
165. Ibid.
166. Douglass C. North, op. cit., pp. 9, 67, and 69.
167. Juan Carlos Casas, *Nuevos políticos y nuevas políticas en América latina*, Editorial Atlántida, Buenos Aires, 1991, p. 7.
168. Index of Economic Freedom, The Heritage Foundation, D.C. 2005 p. 18.
169. Ramón O. Frediani, *Planes de estabilización y reforma estructural en América latina*, (CIEDLA), Fundación Konrad Adenauer, *Buenos Aires*, 1995, p. 15.
170. Robert Gwartney, Robert Lawson, and Walter Block, *Economic Freedom of the World. 1975–1995*, The Fraser Institute, Vancouver, 2004.
171. Secretaría de Programación Económica, Ministerio de Economía y Obras y Servicios Públicos, *Argentina en crecimiento. Los resultados de la reforma económica,1989–1992*, Buenos Aires, 1992, p. 16.
172. Aaron Tornell, "Are Economic Crises Necessary for Trade Liberalization and Fiscal Reform? The Mexican Experience," in Rudiger Dornbusch and Sebastian Edwards (eds.), *Reform, Recovery and Growth. Latin America and the Middle East*, The University of Chicago Press, 1995, p. 54.
173. Aaron Tornell, op. cit., p. 57.
174. Armando Ribas and Eliot Kalter, "The 1994 Mexican Economic Crisis. The Role of Government and Relative Prices," Fondo Monetario Internacional, working paper, November 1999.
175. Armando Ribas, "Del democratismo al dogmatismo en el mercado," working paper.
176. "A basic explanation is that since public spending rises faster than the nominal exchange rate (generally suppressed by antiinflationary measures), spending increases in real terms. Given that public spending is essentially a consumption expense—and we assume it is financed through taxes and debt—an increase in spending increases consumption and reduces savings.

Higher aggregate demand has different effects on markets that compete with exports and on those that for technical reasons do not compete with imports, such as services, construction, etc. The higher demand will have an impact on the markets for tradable goods, i.e., higher aggregate demand will mean an increase in demand for tradable goods without altering prices that are fixed by the exchange rate and lower tariffs. Imports will rise and deficit is created in the current accounts balance (trade balance-debt interest+/-financial services).

However, the impact on non-tradable goods affects both prices and quantities. That is to say, since by definition non-tradable goods cannot be imported, an increase in demand must be satisfied entirely by the supply. If there are restrictions to supply and barriers to entry, which is generally the case, the adjustment will be made through a price increase. This explains why the inflation rate has been observed to be higher for non-tradable goods than for tradable ones.

The different reaction of the price for tradable and non-tradable goods distorts relative prices. In fact, wages and other costs increase in terms of the tradable goods. That is, for producers of goods that compete with exports, costs increase in real terms" (see Armando Ribas and Eliot Kalter, op. cit.).

177. Armando Ribas and Eliot Kalter, op. cit., and Armando Ribas, "Informe de la situación política y económica," September 1999, working paper.

178. North, op. cit., p. 17.

179. *Ibid.*, p. 19.

180. Mariano Tomassi and Sebastián M. Saiegh, *La nueva economía política: Racionalidad e instituciones*, Eudeba, Buenos Aires, 1998, p. 15.

181. Ludwig von Mises [1927], *Liberalismo*, Unión Editorial, Madrid, 1975, p. 17.

182. Economic Freedom Index, The Heritage Foundation, D.C. 2005, p. 179 (Spanish edition).

183. Cited in Economic Freedom Index 2002 published by The Heritage Foundation, p. 194. Ed. (Spanish edition).

184. Economic Freedom Index 2002, Heritage Foundation, pp. 139–140.

185. Such long-term certainty is unknown in the region except for Mexico. The Chilean reforms have now survived four presidential elections without significant backslides.

186. Economic Freedom Index 2002, Heritage Foundation, D.C. 2005 p. 18.

187. Mario Teijeiro, *¿Qué nos pasó?*, May 24, 2002. Published in the website of Centro de Estudios Públicos at www.cep.org.ar.

188. Mario Teijeiro, *¿Qué nos pasó?*, May 24, 2002. Published in the website of Centro de Estudios Públicos at www.cep.org.ar.

189. This statute stated that the National state could under no circumstance alter the terms agreed to between depositors and financial institutions, and that deposits could not be exchanged for public debt bonds, or other public assets; furthermore, it stated that the national state could not alter the maturities, or postpone payment thereof, nor alter rates agreed, or in any way modify the currency of origin of bank deposits.

190. Mancur Olson, *The Rise and Decline of Nations*, Yale University Press, New Haven and London, 1982, Chapter 4.

191. Gustavo Mammoni, "Medio país sin cobertura social," *Hoy* newspaper, La Plata, Argentina, May 24, 2002.

192. FIEL, "Hacia una nueva organización del federalismo fiscal," Buenos Aires, 1993, p. 11.

193. *Ibid.*, p. 41.

194. Adam Smith, *An Inquiry into the Nature and Causes of the Wealth of Nations*, Book V, Chapter 1, Part third, Article 1. Random House Inc., New York, 1985.

195. James Buchanan, "Federalism and Individual Sovereignty," *Cato Journal*, vol. 15, no. 2–3, The Cato Institute, Washington, D.C. (1996): 260 ff.

196. Jorge Ávila, *Nuevo federalismo fiscal*, Fundación Atlas, Buenos Aires, 2003.

197. Jorge M. Capitanich, "Federalismo fiscal y coparticipación federal. Una propuesta para la transformación de la relación nación-provincias," Fundación pro Universidad de la Producción y el Trabajo, Buenos Aires, 1999, p. 33ff.

198. Jorge Ávila, *Nuevo federalismo fiscal*.

199. Roberto Cachanosky, "Las asimetrías entre recaudación y gasto público dan lugar a un federalismo a medias," *La Nación*, February 24, 2002.

200. James M. Buchanan, "Federalism and Individual Sovereignty."

201. Wallace E. Oates, *Federalismo fiscal*, Instituto de Estudios Latinoamericanos, Madrid, 1997.

202. Ehtisham Ahmad and Eric Mottu, "Oil Revenue Assignment: Country Experiences and Issues," International Monetary Fund, November 2002.

203. Gustavo Lazzari and Martín Simonetta, "Mapa del Voto Cautivo en la Argentina," Fundación Atlas, Buenos Aires, Argentina, July 2004.

204. Andrés Oppenheimer, "El peligroso

aumento del voto cautivo," *El Nuevo Herald* (July 2, 2004) and *Miami Herald* (July 1, 2004).

205. Luis Reinaldo Fernández, "De una Urbanización Explosiva a las Ciudades Sustentables." Published in www.ambiente-ecológico.com.ar.

206. Martín Simonetta, "Inserción argentina en la economía mundial" in *Soluciones de Políticas Públicas para un País en Crisis*, Fundación Atlas, Buenos Aires, Argentina, 2003.

207. In Argentina "enganche" means that salary increases at the top of ministries or certain administrative agencies extend to all lower employees as well. This entails conflict particularly in the case of judicial employees.

208. There have been instances of a sort of hereditary employment, where the sons of employees of SEGBA (the electrical distribution corporation) were given priority for positions at the state-owned corporation.

209. In Argentina's national Congress, more than a handful of waiters and drivers have a higher salary than department heads. Seniority accounts for this.

210. Marcel Prelot, *Historia de las ideas políticas*, Buenos Aires: Editorial La Ley, 1971, p. 118.

211. Armando Ribas, *Entre la libertad y la servidumbre*, Stockcero, 2004, pp. 190 and 205.

212. Marcel Prelot, op. cit., p. 480.

213. Armando Ribas, *Entre la libertad y la servidumbre*, pp. 129, 134.

214. Robert A. Peterson, "A Tale of Two Revolutions," *The Freeman: Ideas on Liberty*. Irvington-on-Hudson, New York, August 1989.

215. Samuel Eliot Morison, *The Oxford History of the American People*, New York: Oxford University Press, 1965, p. 182. Quoted in Robert Peterson, above.

216. George Charles Roche, *Frederic Bastiat: A Man Alone*, New Rochelle, N.Y.: Arlington House, 1971, pp. 146–147. Quoted in Robert Peterson, above.

217. Armando Ribas, *¿Quién es Occidente?*, Buenos Aires-Mexico: Editorial Atlántida, 1997, pp. 43, 52.

218. FIEL, *Hacia una nueva organización del federalismo fiscal*, Buenos Aires, 1993, p. 11.

219. *Ibid.*, p. 41.

220. James Buchanan, "Federalism and Individual Sovereignty," *CATO Journal*, vol. 15, no. 2–3, The Cato Institute, Washington, D.C. (1996): 260ff.

Bibliography

Alberdi, Juan B. *Escritos póstumos*. Buenos Aires: Universidad Nacional de Quilmes, 1996.

———. *Sistema económico y rentístico de la Confederación Argentina según su Constitución de 1853*. Buenos Aires: Editorial Raigal, 1954.

Alemann, Roberto T. *Breve historia de la política económica argentina 1500–1989*. Buenos Aires: Editorial Claridad, 1990.

Benegas Lynch (h), Alberto. "Los papeles Antifederalistas." *Libertas* 10 (May 1989).

Bobbio, Norberto, and Nicola Matteucci. *Diccionario de ciencia política*. Mexico: Siglo XXI Editores, 1986.

Borgeaud, Charles. *Établissement et révision des constitutions en Amérique et en Europe*. Paris: Thorin et Fils, 1893.

Buchanan, James. "Federalism and Individual Sovereignty." *Cato Journal*, vol. 15, no. 2–3 (1996).

Bustamante, Jorge E. *Desregulación. Entre el derecho y la economía*. Buenos Aires: Abeledo Perrot, 1993.

Cárdenas Nannetti, Jorge. *Los Estados Unidos, ayer y hoy*. Buenos Aires: Grupo Editorial Norma, 1998.

Cardoso, Fernando Henrique, "Desarrollo y dependencia: Perspectivas teóricas en el análisis sociológico." In *Sociología del desarrollo*. Buenos Aires: Ediciones Solar, 1970.

Casas, Juan Carlos. *Nuevos políticos y nuevas políticas en América latina*. Buenos Aires: Editorial Atlántida, 1991.

Coatsworth, John H. "Obstacles to Economic Growth in Nineteenth Century Mexico." *American Historical Review* 83 (1978).

Cortés Conde, Roberto. *Progreso y declinación de la economía argentina*. Buenos Aires: Fondo de Cultura Económica, 1998.

De Roover, Florence E. "Early Examples of Marine Insurance." *Journal of Economic History* 5 (1977).

De Vries, Jan. *The Economy in Europe in an Age of Crisis, 1600–1750*. Cambridge: Cambridge University Press, 1976.

Dicey, A. V. *Introduction to the Study of the Law of the Constitution*. New York: Macmillan, 1961.

Di Marco, Luis E. "Pensamiento económico de Prebisch." In *Economía internacional y desarrollo: Estudios en honor de Raúl Prebisch*. Buenos Aires: Ediciones Depalma, 1974.

Dornbush, Rudiger, and Sebastian Edwards (eds.). *Reform, Recovery and Growth. Latin America and the Middle East*. Chicago: The University of Chicago Press, 1995.

Duverger, Maurice. *Instituciones políticas y derecho constitucional*. Barcelona: Editorial Ariel, 1984.

ECLAC. *Estudio económico de América latina 1949*. New York: 1951.

Elliot, J. D. "The Decline of Spain." *Past and Present* 20 (November 1961).

Faulkner, Harold U. *American Economic History*. New York: Harper and Brothers, 1935.

A Federalist. "General Introduction: A Dangerous Plan of Benefit only to the 'Aristocratick Combination.'" (1787.) *The Antifederalist Papers*, selected and ed. by Morton Borden. http://www.constitution.org/afp/borden00.htm.

FIEL. *Hacia una nueva organización del federalismo fiscal*. Buenos Aires: 1993.

Frediani, Ramón O. *Planes de estabilización y reforma estructural en América latina*. Buenos Aires: Centro Interdisciplinario de Estudios sobre el Desarrollo Latinoamericano (CIEDLA), Fundación Konrad Adenauer, 1995.

Galeano, Eduardo. *Las venas abiertas de América Latina*, Editorial del Chanchito. Montevideo, 1996.

García Hamilton, José I. *El autoritarismo hispanoamericano y la improductividad*. Buenos Aires: Editorial Sudamericana, 1998.

Gettel, Raymond G. *Political Science*. Vol. 1. Boston: Ginn, 1949.

Glade, William P. *The Latin American Economies: A Study of Their Institutional Evolution*. New York: American Book, 1969.

Gondra, Luis Roque. *Estudios de historia y economía*. Buenos Aires: Imprenta de la Universidad, 1938.

Gorostiaga, Norberto. *Recurso extraordinario ante la Corte Suprema de la Nación: orígenes históricos*. Buenos Aires: 1944.

Grondona, Mariano. *Las condiciones culturales del desarrollo económico. Hacia una teoría del desarrollo*. Buenos Aires: Editorial Planeta, 1999.

Guerrero, Alexander. *Todo el Petróleo para el Fisco*. Published on the Website of CEDICE, Venezuela.

Guiddens, Anthony. *The Protestant Ethics and the Spirit of Capitalism*. Foreword by Max Weber. London: George Allen & Unwin Ltd., 1976.

Gwartney, Robert, Robert Lawson, and Walter Block. *Economic Freedom of the World, 1975–1990*. Vancouver: The Fraser Institute, 1996.

Halperín Donghi, Tulio. *Historia contemporánea de América latina*. Buenos Aires: Alianza Editorial, 1994.

Harrison, Lawrence E. *El sueño panamericano*. Buenos Aires: Editorial Ariel, 1999.

Holmes, Oliver W., Jr. *The Common Law*, Boston: Little, Brown, 1938.

Johnson, John J. *Militares y sociedad en América latina*. Buenos Aires: Ediciones Solar-Hachette S.A., 1966.

Kñákal, Jan, and Aníbal Pinto. "El sistema centro-periferia 20 años después." In *Economía internacional y desarrollo: Estudios en honor de Raúl Prebisch*. Buenos Aires: Ediciones Depalma, 1974.

Landes, David S. *La riqueza y la pobreza de las naciones*. Buenos Aires: Vergara, 1999.

Las Casas, Bartolomé de. *Historia de las Indias*, Vol. 3, Ch. 4. Barcelona: Plaza & Janés, 1929.

Linares Quintana, Segundo V. *Derecho constitucional e instituciones políticas*. Buenos Aires: Ed. Plus Ultra, 1981.

Llach, Juan José. *Otro siglo, otra Argentina*. Buenos Aires: Editorial Ariel, 1997.

Locke, John. *Two Treatises of Government*. Cambridge: Cambridge University Press, 1988.

López, Robert S., and Irving W. Raymond. *Medieval Trade in the Mediterranean*. New York: Columbia University Press, 1955.

Lynch, John. *The Spanish American Revolutions, 1808–1826*. New York: Norton, 1986.

Mammoni, Gustavo. "Medio país sin cobertura social." *Hoy* (La Plata, Argentina), May 24, 2003.

Mecham, J. Lloyd. *Church and State in Latin America: A History of Politico-Ecclesiastical Relations*. Chapel Hill: University of North Carolina Press, 1966.

Mises, Ludwig von [1927]. *Liberalismo*. Madrid: Unión Editorial, 1975.

Mitchell, William. *An Essay on the Early History of the Law Merchant*. New York: Burt Franklin Press, 1969.

Montaner, Carlos, et al. *Fabricantes de miseria*. Barcelona: Plaza & Janés, 1998.

Morison, Samuel, Henry Commager and William Leuchtenburg. *A Concise*

History of the American Republic. New York: Oxford University Press, 1977.

Mrad, M. Gabriela. "El *common law* en la tradición del orden espontáneo." *Libertas* 12 (May 1990).

North, Douglass C. *Institutions, Institutional Change and Economic Performance*, Cambridge: Cambridge University Press, 1990.

O'Grady, Mary. "First Open Markets." In *Index of Economic Freedom 2002.* Washington, DC: The Heritage Foundation, 2002.

Olson, Mancur. *The Rise and Decline of Nations.* Yale University Press, New Haven: 1982.

Paz, Octavio. *The Labyrinth of Solitude and Other Writings.* New York: Grove Press, 1985.

Phillips; Chalmers; and Hood [first names unknown]. *Constitutional Laws of Great Britain, the British Empire and the Commonwealth*, 6th edition. London: Sweet and Maxwell Ltd., 1946.

Popescu, Oreste. *Estudios en la historia del pensamiento económico latinoamericano.* Bogota: Plaza & Janés, 1986.

Ramella, Pablo A. *Derecho constitucional.* Buenos Aires: Ediciones Depalma, 1986.

Rawley, Charles. "Institutional Choice and Public Choice." In *The Revolution in Development Economics* by James A. Dorn. Washington DC: The Cato Institute, 1998.

Ribas, Armando. "Del democratismo al dogmatismo en el mercado." Working Paper.

_____. "Entre la libertad y servidumbre." Buenos Aires: Stockero, 2004.

Ribas, Armando, and Eliot Kalter. "The 1994 Mexican Economic Crisis: The Role of Government and Relative Prices." International Monetary Fund, Working Paper, November 1999.

Roberts, Paul Craig, and Karen Lafollette Araujo. *The Capitalist Revolution in Latin America.* New York: Oxford University Press, 1997.

Rock, David. *Argentina 1516–1982: From Spanish Colonization to the Falklands War.* Berkeley: University of California Press, 1985.

Rojas, Ricardo M. "El orden jurídico espontáneo." *Libertas* 13 (October 1990).

Roll, Eric. *Historia de las doctrinas económicas.* Mexico: Fondo de Cultura Económica, 1994.

Sabine, George H. *Historia de la teoría política.* Mexico: Fondo de Cultura Económica, 1963.

Salas, Alberto M. *Las armas de la conquista.* Buenos Aires: Emecé Editores, 1950.

Secretaría de Programación Económica, Ministerio de Economía y Obras y Servicios Públicos, *Argentina en crecimiento. Los resultados de la reforma económica, 1989–1992.* Buenos Aires: 1992.

Shenfield, Arthur. "Hayek y el derecho." In *Libertas* 7 (October 1987).

Smith, Adam. *An Inquiry into the Nature and Causes of the Wealth of Nations.* New York: Random House, 1985.

Soto Hernando de. *The Other Path. The Invisible Revolution in the Third World.* New York: Harper & Row, 1989.

Stepan, Alfred. *Rethinking Military Politics: Brazil and the Southern Cone.* Princeton: Princeton University Press, 1988.

Teijeiro, Mario, *¿Qué nos pasó?* Published on the Website of Centro de Estudios Públicos at www.cep.org.ar.

Tomassi, Mariano, and Sebastián M. Saiegh. *La nueva economía política: Racionalidad e instituciones.* Buenos Aires: Eudeba, 1998.

Tullock, Gordon. "The Backward Society: Static Inefficiency, Rent Seeking and The Rule of Law." In *The Theory of Public Choice II*, ed. by James M. Buchanan and Robert D. Tollison. Ann Arbor: The University of Michigan, 1984.

Vacchino, Juan M. *Integración latinoamericana. De la ALALC a la ALADI.* Buenos Aires: Ediciones Depalma, 1983.

Vazquez, Ian. *Está la economía mexicana preparada para despegar?* Washington, DC: Cato Institute.

_____. *Una política exterior de Estados Unidos para America Latina.* Washington, DC: Cato Institute.

Véliz, Claudio. *The Centralist Tradition of Latin America*. Princeton, NJ: Princeton University Press, 1982.

Vicens Vives, Jaime. *An Economic History of Spain*. Princeton, NJ: Princeton University Press, 1969.

Wright, Ione S., and Lisa M. Nekhom. *Diccionario histórico argentino*. Buenos Aires: Emecé Editores, 1990.

Yeatts, Guillermo M. *Subsurface Wealth: The Struggle for Privatization in Argentina*. The Foundation for Economic Education [FEE], Irvington-on-Hudson, NY: 1997.

Index

Adelantados 41
Ahmad, Ehtisham 143
Alberdi, Juan Bautista 2
Alexander III 32
Alexander VI (Pope) 37
Alphonse I (King) 20
Antifederalist 58, 59, 60
Apuleyo, Plinio 10
Artaza, Nito 121
Austin, Stephan F. 62
Ávila, Jorge 135

Bastiat, Frédéric 15, 120, 155
Berkley, John 47
Bill of Rights 18, 57, 58, 68
Bobbio, Norberto 81
Bolívar, Simón 52
Buchanan, James 12, 123, 126, 131, 138, 159
Bustamante, Jorge 33

Cabot, John 44
Cachanosky, Roberto 136
Calvers, Cecil 47
Calvin, John 32
Capitulación 158, 164
Captive vote 144, 145
Cárdenas Nannetti, Jorge 44
Cardoso, Fernando Henrique 4
Carteret, George 47
Casas, Juan Carlos 84, 85
Center-periphery theory 78
Cesarino Junio, A. F. 74
Charles V 22
Civilian-military pendulum 80
Clinton, George 60
Coatsworth, John 41
Codes 8, 24, 25, 34, 36
Common Law 24, 25, 26

Convertibility 117, 119, 120, 122, 123, 124, 142
Cortes 20, 23
Cortés, Hernán 35, 38
Cortés Conde, Roberto 54, 68, 88
Cromwell, Oliver 25, 26

Degollado, Santos 2
de la Rúa, Fernando 108, 120, 124, 127
de las Casas, Bartolomé 40, 41
de Montesinos, Fray Antonio 39, 40, 41
de San Martín, José 52, 53
de Soto, Hernando 15
De Vries, Jan 21
Díaz, Porfirio 2
Dicey, A.V. 23
Distribution of rents 13, 96
Distributional coalitions 126
Don Pedro I 63
Donghi, Halperín 51, 54, 64, 69
Duhalde, Eduardo 120, 123, 124, 125
Duke of York 47
Duverger, Maurice 76, 83

Economic statism 2, 3, 10
Edwards, Sebastián 89, 91
Elizabeth I (Queen) 44
Elliot, J. 22
Encomienda 38, 39, 40, 41
Establish rights 25, 26

Faulkner, Harold U. 43, 45
Federalist 55, 58, 59, 61, 68, 69, 70
Floria, Carlos 50
Fueros 20, 21
Fujimori, Alberto 101

Galeano, Eduardo 78, 79
García, Juan Agustín 2, 4

García Hamilton, José Ignacio 10, 19, 35, 38, 52
General will 153, 154, 156
Gilbert, Sir Humphrey 44
Glade, William 53, 64, 66, 68
Glorious Revolution 18, 27, 68, 152, 154, 155
González, Felipe 89
Gorges, Ferdinand 46
Gorostiaga, Norberto 21
Grondona, Mariano 10
Guerrero, Alexander 106

Hanke, Steve 121
Harrison, Lawrance 10
Hayek, Friedrich von 8, 13, 26, 160
Holmes, Oliver W. 24

Individual rights 21, 24, 60, 75, 154, 156, 157, 161, 166
Industrialization 64, 73, 78, 79, 81

James II 28
John (King) 25
Johnson, John J. 81, 82
Juárez, Benito 2
Juros 22

Kant, Immanuel 15, 154, 155

La Follette Araujo, Karen 10
Landes, David S. 60
Liberal constitutionalism 74
Liberal democracy 75
Linares Quintana, Segundo 20, 21, 29
Locke, John 16, 26, 27, 28, 153, 154, 156
López, Vicente F. 133
López de Santa Anna, Antonio 2
López Murphy, Ricardo 127
Luther, Martin 28, 29, 30
Lynch, John 49, 50

Magna Carta of 1215 18, 20, 24, 25, 68
Mammoni, Gustavo 126
Martí, José 4
Mason, George 57
Mason, John 46
Matteucci, Nicola 81
Maynard Keynes, John 77
Mecham, Lloyd 62
Menem, Carlos 100, 107
Mesta 21, 22

Mita 38, 39
Montaner, Carlos Alberto 10
Mottu, Eric 143

Nationalism 73, 74, 82
North, Douglass 7, 10, 11, 18, 22, 23, 26, 33, 34, 67, 68, 74, 88, 100, 101, 159

Ocampo, Melchor 2
Oglethorpe, James 47
O'Higgins, Bernardo 52, 63
Olson, Mancur 123, 126
Oppenheimer, Andrés 144, 143

Paz, Octavio 20, 30, 41
Penn, William 46
Perlot, Marcel 154
Peterson, Robert 155
Philip II 22
Philip III 22
Philip IV 21, 22
Piñera, José 112
Pinochet, Augusto 81, 88, 96, 101
Political entrepreneur 101
Political trusteeship 154
Popescu, Oreste 39, 40, 41
Populist regimes 76, 80
Prebisch, Raúl 77, 78
Privatization 7, 14, 87, 88, 92, 93, 94, 95, 96, 97, 99, 101, 110, 117, 159, 163, 164
Profit-seeking behavior 12
Property rights 7, 11, 14, 21, 22, 23, 31, 54, 58, 71, 72, 75, 103, 104, 106, 108, 110, 112, 118, 121, 122, 123, 125, 159, 160, 163, 164
Protect rights 25

Raleigh, Walter 44
Ramos Arizpe, Miguel 62
Rangel, Carlos 4
Rawley, Charles 72, 75
Reason of state 154
Reformation 28, 29, 30, 31
Renán, Ernesto 3
Rent-seeking behavior 12
Repartimiento 38
Ribas, Armando 98, 145, 154, 155, 156
Roberts, Paul Craig 10
Rock, David 11, 42
Rodó, José Enrique 3
Rodríguez Sáa, Adolfo 120, 124
Rojas, Ricardo M. 24, 52
Roll, Eric 32
Rosas, Juan Manuel de 1,

Rousseau, Jean Jacques 154, 156, 157
Rule of law 104, 110, 112, 154

Saiegh, Sebastián 101
Saint Agustin 32
Salas, Alberto M. 38
Sánchez de Lozada, Goni 101, 109
Santa Cruz, Andrés 52
Shernfield, Arthur 8
Social constitutionalism 72, 74, 75, 76
Social democracy 75
Social rights 75, 76, 149, 154
Spencer, Herbert 3,
Stepan, Alfred 81, 82
Stuart, Charles, I 26
Stuart, Charles, II 27
Substitution of market mechanisms 89
Subsurface wealth 7
Sucre, Antonio de 52
Szewach, Enrique 86

Techno-military regimes 83
Teijeiro, Mario 118, 117, 119, 125
Terán, Juan B. 2, 4
Theory of dependence 4, 78

Theory of the two swords 28
Thomas, Robert 11
Tomassi, Mariano 101
Tornell, Aarón 95
Tullock, Gordon 13

Underdeveloped 10, 72, 78, 79, 105
Underground economy 76
Urquiza, Juan Justo de 2

Vacchino, Juan 79
Vargas Llosa, Álvaro 10
Vargas Llosa, Mario 15, 16
Véliz, Claudio 52, 61
Voting with one's feet 154

Wealth creation 12, 13, 31, 33, 69, 98, 150
Weber, Max 29, 30
White indentured servants 45
William of Orange 27
William II 27
Williams, Roger 46

Yanaconazgo 38, 39

www.ingramcontent.com/pod-product-compliance
Ingram Content Group UK Ltd.
Pitfield, Milton Keynes, MK11 3LW, UK
UKHW042015140426
5217IPUK00015B/1186